MOWGLI
STREET FOOD

MOWGLI
STREET FOOD

Stories and recipes from the Mowgli Street Food restaurants

NISHA KATONA

NOURISH
EAT WELL, LIVE WELL

I thank God for my original Mowglis, India and Tia. For Mothers of Mowgli, Maa and Monmon. For Zoltan, for wisdom, for richer for poorer.

'A little sleep, a little slumber, a little folding of the hands to rest, and poverty will come on you like a thief and scarcity like an armed man.'

First published in the UK and USA in 2018 by Nourish, an imprint of Watkins Media Limited
Unit 11, Shepperton House,
89-93 Shepperton Road, London N1 3DF
enquiries@nourishbooks.com

Managing Editor: Kate Fox
Designer: Glen Wilkins
Copyeditor: Kay Delves
Photography: Yuki Sugiura
Food and Prop Stylist: Aya Nishimura

Typeset in Futura
Colour reproduction by XY Digital
Printed in Bosnia and Herzegovina

A CIP record for this book is available from the British Library

ISBN: 978-1-84899-412-6

Publisher's note
While every care has been taken in compiling the recipes for this book, Watkins Media Limited, or any other persons who have been involved in working on this publication, cannot accept responsibility for any errors or omissions, inadvertent or not, that may be found in the recipes or text, nor for any problems that may arise as a result of preparing one of these recipes. If you are pregnant or breastfeeding or have any special dietary requirements or medical conditions, it is advisable to consult a medical professional before following any of the recipes contained in this book.

Notes on the recipes
Unless otherwise stated:
Use medium fruit and vegetables
Use medium (US large) organic or free-range eggs
Use fresh herbs, spices and chillies
Use granulated sugar (Americans can use ordinary granulated sugar when caster sugar is specified)
Do not mix metric, imperial and US cup measurements:
1 tsp = 5ml 1 tbsp = 15ml 1 cup = 240ml

nourishbooks.com

CONTENTS

INTRODUCTION
NISHA KATONA

My life began in Ormskirk, Lancashire, where I was born, the daughter of Indian immigrant doctors. I remember growing up in a house in which every emotion was vociferously expressed, every guest embraced as a member of the family; a house filled with noise, with the aroma of wild exotic cooking and, above all, filled with so much love.

I was then raised in 1970s Skelmersdale – a small town in West Lancashire – where my parents took their first medical practice. This was an entirely white, working class area and it is not an unusual tale of the 1970s immigrant that some of my earliest memories were of being firebombed, of bricks being thrown through our windows and stones aimed at us on the way to school. We had little to offer. We were not cool. We were not rich. It was actually the thing that came most naturally to us that became our saviour – it was our love for hospitality and our open kitchen that became the Kofi Annan of race relations. My mother's generous and gorgeous rolling buffet meant our little Skem home became *the* place for teens to hang out. Their parents followed and my dad strode through acres of Johnnie Walker Black Label on the swaying road to integration. He didn't complain, I promise you.

You see, above all, Indians love to feed people. There is something very humble and uncomplicated about Indian social culture – we aim to please and we want you to like us. Warmth and generosity is beamed down on you like a blinding beacon of love, whether you want it or not. Taking you by the elbow to the kitchen table and setting before you enormous plates of food is the only way to make friends, right? Good hospitality is at the heart of the Indian home and guests are treated like royalty. If you arrived unannounced at my mother's home, within minutes the stove would be fired up and a delicious platter of something yellow and come-hither would be on its way to you. I remember scoffing snacks of tea-steeped chickpeas after school at brave Mr Jagota's shop – one of the only Asian shops in Liverpool at the time – while he shared stories of his own childhood. I recall the dinner table at home heaving with decidedly more dishes than there were people seated around it, everyone talking over each other and sharing out the food among ourselves.

7

So, although there may have been many, many already awkward teenage moments made all the more awkward by the mismatching hand-me-down knitwear, a kitchen full of excruciatingly different food, a distinct lack of Adidas and no shortage of brown corduroy, I am forever, truly and unapologetically grateful for my blushes, because without them, I may never have daydreamed Mowgli into existence.

FROM THE COURTROOM TO THE KITCHEN

My route to the kitchen is perhaps an unusual one. I didn't start off with a desire to work with food, although maybe on some deeper level I did. Like any good Indian daughter, I worked hard at school and passed all my exams. I then went on to become the first female Indian barrister in Liverpool. The law, especially at that time, was a very male-dominated industry and I recall on my first day of mini pupillage being sent a note by the head of chambers that said: 'Tell her not to return tomorrow as she is female and Asian and the bar is no place for such a person.' I surprised myself by returning to chambers the next day. I was more afraid of my mother than of the man at the top of the stagnant ivory tower.

Determination and the knowledge that I would have to work ten times harder than those around me lead on to a thoroughly enjoyable legal career. I was then appointed trustee of the National Museums Liverpool by the Department for Culture, Media and Sport in 2008. And in 2009, the Cabinet Office anointed me Ambassador for Diversity in Public Appointments. I was an 'expert advisor' for the *Guardian*; and I also spoke regularly on the radio – both locally and nationally. I was proud to be giving a voice to women, hopefully at the same time demonstrating to other women that it is possible to succeed in a predominantly male work environment.

But a love of good food and an even greater love of the alchemy at play in the kitchen awoke in me the call to cooking; a call that I simply could not ignore. And as is so often the story with those of us who end up working in the food industry, those heady, bewitching scents of the kitchen kept pulling me back.

When not practising law, I lived the life of a fully fledged foodie. Holidays were booked solely around the local food offerings – China, Vietnam, Morocco, Italy, South Korea – and I became almost infatuated with sharing my new discoveries with anyone I could seat at my kitchen table for long enough. At night, I conjured up new dishes, marrying new discoveries with the long-held and well-learnt traditions from my family's own handwritten recipes. I became a curry evangelist, giving lessons in the ancient curry formulas of India.

It is obvious though, I think, that curry house offerings on most British high streets are unrecognisable to most Indians. Ask an Indian for a balti and

they will bring you a bucket; tikka masala was born out of a Glaswegian man's love of gravy on his chicken; and passanda translates as 'I like,' as in 'chicken, I like'.

As I delved further, researched more, I kept asking myself, where was the authentic Indian home-cooking? The hugely varied, fresh, delicately spiced, healthy dishes enjoyed at lunch and dinner by Indian families around the world? British palates, at least until recently, seemed to be geared up to reject anything that did not involve chunks of meat floating in a neon sauce.

One reason for the lack of home-style cooking on the high street perhaps lies in the fact that traditional Indian cooking does not revolve around meat. In Britain, pulses used to be seen as mostly the preserve of hippies and those with gastrointestinal complaints. But Indian cooking is at its most magical in its cooking of vegetables, and what a varied, wonderful magic trick it is.

It felt time to share these ancient recipes; passed on by my ancestors, eaten at home, on the street, packed up and taken to work. To bring real Indian food to the masses. And so, although I had loved every single day of my 20 years at the Bar, and felt an enormous sense of pride in helping my clients – the children and victims of neglect, abuse and domestic violence – I couldn't escape those temptress tastes of far-flung lands any longer.

I used all my savings, all my inheritance, every bit of security I had and I began negotiations with Liverpool One – a slick shopping complex in the centre of town. No surprise here that I lost out on the site to a sweet donut concept. Who would take a risk on an unestablished independent peddling her mother's recipes, when they had the sure-fire hit and covenant strength of the sugar-coated, deep-fried all-American dream?

Undeterred, I looked further out, to the bohemian and artistic neighbourhoods on the fringes of Liverpool. And the rest, as they say, is history. We set up Mowgli Bold Street and within weeks the queues formed, much to my absolute surprise. It was then that I realised that Mowgli was a thing much bigger than me. That I was a trustee of this living, sassy, independent creature and that she would teach me how she needed to be led. And she wanted to be led across the nation. It was then, watching the queues and watching my team of incredible, dedicated staff, that I felt duplicitous in continuing to practise as a barrister. Three months after Mowgli was born, I took a sabbatical and turned to face the new life in front of me.

MOWGLI

Mowgli is based on the way that Indians eat at home and on their streets: fresh, zingy, hectic, colourful flavours. But calling it 'street food' loses some of itself in translation and suggests something far less than it is. Street food in the whole of the East is a far cry from the ubiquitous strap line we overuse in the West. The majority of the world's population does not revolve around a restaurant culture, but around a street food culture. Indian eating when not done at home is most often practised outside, on the street, on the move, chatting to people around you. Each vendor sells his speciality, borne of years of honing his skills into one perfect dish. Bhajis of courgette flowers, densely battered and beautifully spiced; cones of roasted chickpeas, devoured by everyone from businessmen to children dawdling on their way home from school; delicately aromatic curries served in banana leaf bowls. All of these are recreated in the pages of this book.

For the Mowgli Menu, I chose my favourite 20 Indian dishes, irrespective of region. I chose the dishes that I am addicted to. The dishes I have to eat twice a week to avoid going cold turkey. It turns out we have 20 dishes with only 8 meat dishes. The menu at Mowgli is all about the food Indians actually eat. The stuff that goes on the stove once the guests have left – humble, undressed, light fare.

The stuff we think our English visitors would hate because it is not comprised of lumps of meat floating in a rich gravy. I take a huge risk with the Mowgli menu. Dishes like Temple Dahl are such a far cry from the heavy tarka dahls of the takeaways. Mowgli's guests need to recalibrate their expectations of Indian food. Calcutta Tangled Greens and House Lamb Curry, Tea-Steeped Chickpeas and soft party Puris... these are the dishes you find cold in an Indian's refrigerator, dormant, waiting, full of virtuosic flavour. This is the stuff of Mowgli.

I never contrived the Mowgli menu to have a particular vegan–meat balance. I simply chose the best dishes I know and it was a shocking moment when I performed the tally. I never wanted it this way. Commercial pressures would dictate a meat-heavy menu. But in that moment of crafting the finished menu, it was almost as though the food had animated me to write it. I was subconsciously awakening the food of my ancestors and once invoked, its face was quite unrecognisable. This was not a menu like any curry house I know. Suddenly the meat section looked like a minority pursuit. It overturns the balance that we have in the West where a meal must be based around meat. The Mowgli menu is how Indians eat at home and if you want to partake, everything about it will take you out of your curry comfort zone.

The dishes served at Mowgli are based around the Indian culture of 'chat', which translates as 'lick' (as in, 'lick one's plate clean'). Every day in Indian homes and at street stalls, chat is served in small portions of explosive flavour meant for sharing. Mixing plates creates perfect combinations of taste and texture –

bright fresh coriander, the sweet-sour tang of tamarind, spicy-cool yogurt and a satisfying gram flour crunch.

I love spice – it is an addiction for me. Not so much the fiery chilli that seems beloved by British palates, but the aromatic, subtly powerful headnotes of spices like cardamom, cumin and nigella seeds. I enjoy creating pure explosions of taste in every mouthful – contrasting but complementary textures and flavours that can almost overwhelm, but are then pulled back and tempered at the last minute, cooled and refreshed. I love food you can get involved in, to pick up with your hands, to share, to steal off each other's plates. Eating together should be an assault on all the senses – the noise, the colour, the smells and the textures – doing away with restraint and table-clothed British sensitivities. Mowgli is for me the vibrancy of an eatery, the mess, the lively Indian home of my teen years, a bustling Indian night market at lunchtime 4,000 miles away.

Food reflects the times we live in and I feel that right now is an overwhelmingly exciting time; a time in which most people – at least in the world of food of which I am now an honoured part – are open to welcoming new ideas and tastes from abroad. I eat at Mowgli twice a day, so the food you eat when you're there really is the food I eat too. I'm constantly hanging around in the kitchen, annoying my marvellous team of chefs, mixing, meddling and trying out new ideas – some happy accidents and some careful culinary adventures. Many a happy mash-up of my Indian and British food life have happened this way.

The Mowgli menu and this cookbook is my list of desert island dishes. These are the dishes I need, of which I have never tired; these dishes tell the tales of my life and they taste of the love of my family.

TIFFIN

The food of Mowgli is the food of the tiffin carrier lunch. The best Indian food is forged for lunchtime trade. This is when the food-roulette tiffin tins tell you if you are in the good books with your spouse; whether your mum had you down for a jam or spam day.

When office workers in India leave home for work, they cannot take with them their home-cooked hot lunches. Their lunches follow them in stacked tiffin tins, by train, mule, taxi and turban. The billion-dollar industry of tiffin carriers even wait and return the washing up home. Children are sent to school with their bright tiffin carriers full of light, flavourful, vegetarian dishes designed to be easily digested and to freshen the mind.

One of the charms of tiffin is the moment of the reveal. The recipient does not know what they are going to get until they lift the lid. It will be different every day, but the dishes will all be light, fragrant and full of home-cooked flavour – the tastes of Mowgli.

THE MOWGLI MONKEY

I came to Mowgli late, a dowager tiger mother of monkeys. I designed every brick of Mowgli, every element of her physicality. I laboured ridiculously over her, and always will. Not one shelf goes up without me pondering it and positioning it. I wanted to create a place that neutralised your expectations entirely, that removed all those preconceptions you would have of an Indian restaurant so that we could then do to you what we wanted with our food. I used the temples behind my grandmother's Varanasi home as the palette for my design. Broken-down grandeur, warm, worn brick hung about with vines, monkeys with their sass and their independent determination striding across the rooftops. The Monkey logo was borne from those memories. I still remember the whole-body thrill I felt seeing the Mowgli Monkey being carried down Oxford Street on a tote bag in London when we were just one restaurant strong. She strides before me does this monkey. With her ponderous frown and her defiant flick of the tail. She is the personification of all that I have built.

MOWGLI, THE COOKBOOK

From between these pages and then at home around your own table, I hope you will join me on my culinary journey as it diverts and digresses, twists back on itself and finally comes together as a collection of tried-and-tested dishes, kindled on the home fires of my ancestors and carried across the ages and the oceans in the hearts of those I love.

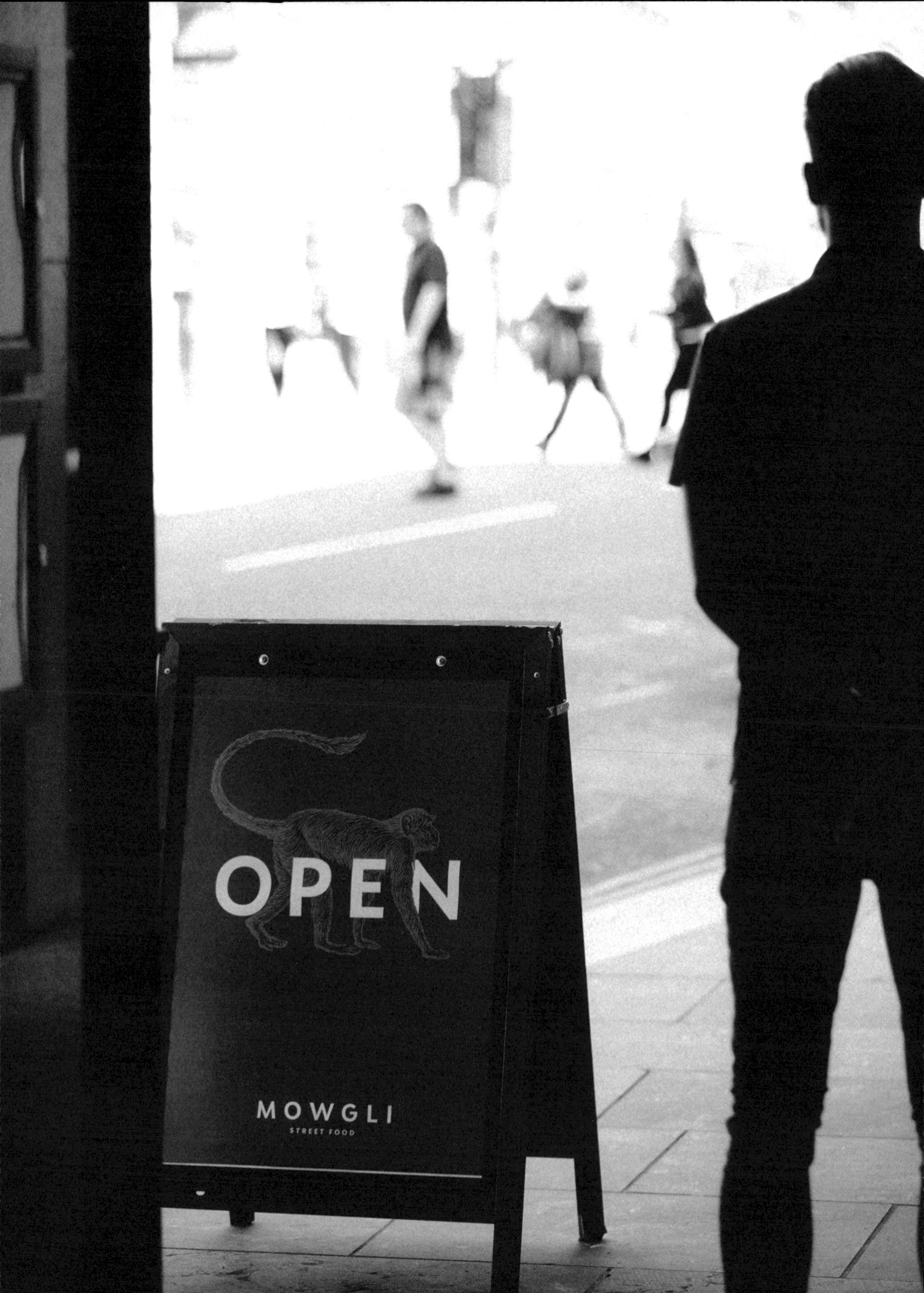
OPEN
MOWGLI
STREET FOOD

1

STREET
CHAT

The street chat section of our menu is the reason I built Mowgli. It is the way that Indians eat day in, day out in every corner of their lives: from schools and railways to offices. It is the reason I chose the title Mowgli Street Food and, since then, the sudden proliferation of this phrase irks me daily, but should it?

Food is a little like fashion. There are fads that are bang on trend, there are timeless classics, there is the readily forgiven ethnic scene and the crushingly difficult haute couture of Michelin aspiration.

And, like fashion, certain genres inspire jaded disdain at any one moment. The ra-ra skirt, the slanket and the onesie of the food world now seem to be the concepts of dirty food, pulled pork and, sadly for me, street food.

It is very easy to roll one's eyes at the ubiquitous 'street food', but are we being too quick to judge? Are these genres of food in fact timeless, simply adding to the colours of the ever brightening food scene? It is this question that keeps me up at night. I built Mowgli Street Food only 3 years ago and yet, night after night, I ponder the need to remove the words 'street food' from our title.

Mowgli is a pet name I called my children. For me, it is a soft, round word filled with love. Street food, that thorny phrase, is to me the way a billion Indians eat every day.

In fact it's not just Indians that eat like this. Street food is the daily dining experience of the majority of the world's population.

The restaurant is an eating construct of the cold and wealthy West. In the East, food has a brisker, more focused, more intense articulation. In the heat of the East, workers and diners do not want to sit inside a stuffy building filled with cooking fumes. Air conditioning, refrigeration, complex kitchen equipment and expensive overheads are no match for talented food pedlars selling their signature dishes from open stalls on the world's chaotic and peopled pavements.

Street food is a concept almost as old as the foundations of the Earth – or at least civilization. It was a concept born as soon as currency and community breathed their first. So street food is to the food world what shoes are to fashion – infinitely varied, but ultimately ubiquitous. And like shoes, where you can spend thousands on a pair of Choos or rely on your humble chappals, street food may have been hijacked by the trendy, but it will always be an honest necessity too.

For me, and for Mowgli, thankfully, whichever way I look at it, street food has legs, and in a good way. I hope for all of us that the informal, honest, smash-and-grab, big-flavoured concept of the world street food scene is going nowhere.

19

MOWGLI CHIP BUTTY

PREP: 5 MINUTES • COOK: 20 MINUTES • SERVES 4

Indians who live across the world cannot help but pimp local dishes to make them taste more Indian. Spice is a drug for us. We can go a couple of days on bangers and mash but then we start to sneak adulterants into our grub to get that spice hit. Whenever we brought chips into our home, if we turned our back on them, my mother would have done this chip butty thing to them. This involved red onion, green chilli and a hot pickle in a roti wrap. It drove me and my brother mad, but we loved it. This is one of our big sellers, so well done Maa.

5 large Maris Piper potatoes, cut into
   1cm/½ inch cubes
2 tsp ground turmeric
salt
4 tbsp vegetable oil
2 tbsp finely chopped red onion
2½ tsp chat masala

2 tsp ground coriander
2 tbsp roughly chopped fresh
   coriander/cilantro
4 tbsp Green Chilli Pickle (see
   page 146)
4 Rotis (see page 130)
4 tbsp Mowgli Chutney (see page 147)

1 In a large saucepan set over a medium-high heat, add the chopped potatoes, a pinch of salt and the ground turmeric and cover with cold water. Bring up to the boil, then reduce the heat to low and simmer for 8–10 minutes or until the potatoes become soft but still hold together. Drain well and set aside.

2 In a large non-stick frying pan set over a medium-high heat, add the vegetable oil. When hot, add the drained potatoes and fry for 8 minutes, stirring regularly, until golden brown and crisp.

3 Put the potatoes into a large bowl and add the red onion, chat masala, ground coriander, fresh coriander, green chilli pickle and ½ teaspoon salt and toss well until everything is fully combined.

4 Lay each roti out on a flat work surface, then spread a tablespoon of the Mowgli chutney down the middle of each. Spoon equal amounts of the fried potatoes onto the Mowgli chutney, then carefully roll each roti tightly. Using a sharp knife cut each chip butty in half, then serve with the remaining fried potatoes.

MASALA OMELETTE WRAP

Wow, the power of social media cannot be understated. Nor can its absolute usefulness in being able to turn a business like Mowgli around on a dime. The omelette wrap is a very common Indian meal. We have it at breakfast, lunch, dinner or supper. It is a delicious, oozing dish, but it sold terribly. I put the question out on Facebook as to why it was unpopular – had it been flavour, I would have pulled it off the menu. The feedback was instant. No one in England wants to go to a restaurant and order a dish with the word 'omelette' in it. Overnight it became the Mowgli masala wrap and the sales trebled. This is one of our staff favourites.

50g/2oz/½ cup grated cheddar cheese

½ tsp ground coriander

¼ tsp ground cumin

1 tsp chopped fresh coriander/cilantro

2 tbsp vegetable oil

¼ red onion, finely sliced

1 small red chilli, deseeded and finely sliced

2 eggs

pinch of salt

1 chapati

1 tbsp Mowgli Chutney (see page 147)

1 Preheat your grill/broiler. Mix together the grated cheese, ground coriander, ground cumin and fresh coriander and set aside.

2 Put the vegetable oil in a small non-stick frying pan and set over a medium heat. When hot, add the red onion and red chilli and fry for 4 minutes or until the onion is soft and translucent.

3 Whisk the eggs lightly with a fork, then pour into the pan and give everything a quick mix. Season with the salt and cook gently until the eggs are just set, then sprinkle the cheese mixture on top of the eggs and place under the grill/broiler. Grill/broil for 3–4 minutes or until the cheese is bubbling and golden.

4 Take your chapati and spoon on the Mowgli chutney, then carefully slide the cooked omelette out of the pan and on top of the chapati. Roll tightly, slice in half at an angle and serve immediately.

HIMALAYAN CHEESE ON TOAST

This is one of Mowgli's most popular dishes. To get our spice kick, Indians pimp up English staples with three cardinal ingredients: coriander/cilantro, onion and green chilli. You can throw these into a Pot Noodle and make it Indian, I swear. Coriander gives a herby, floral note and the chilli and onions, a sharp sweetness. These additional tones wake up the heavy ooze of the cheese and you really need a good, strong cheddar to take the assault of the spice.

1 tsp vegetable oil

½ tsp cumin seeds

50g/2oz/½ cup grated extra-mature cheddar cheese

½ tsp ground coriander

¼ tsp ground cumin

½ small red onion, finely diced

1 small green chilli, deseeded and finely sliced

1 tbsp roughly chopped fresh coriander/cilantro, plus extra to serve

2.5cm/1 inch thick piece of white bread

1 Preheat your grill/broiler. Put the vegetable oil in a small non-stick saucepan and set over a medium heat. When hot, add the cumin seeds and fry until they turn dark brown and fragrant, then set aside.

2 In a small bowl mix together the grated cheese, ground coriander, ground cumin, red onion, green chilli, fresh coriander and the fried cumin seeds. Put your bread on a baking sheet and toast on each side, taking care not to burn.

3 Carefully sprinkle the cheese mixture onto one side of the toast and grill/broil for 3 minutes or until the cheese is bubbling and golden brown.

4 Finish with a little more fresh coriander and serve immediately.

TREACLE TAMARIND FRIES

PREP: 5 MINUTES • COOK: 20 MINUTES • SERVES 4–6

I eat in Mowgli twice a day. I am forever in the kitchen looking at new permutations and combinations of what lies within to perk up my lunch. I found myself often going in to chat to the chefs, dipping the Fenugreek Kissed Fries (see page 28) into the sauce of the Tamarind Treacle Ribs (see page 56). This is how this dish evolved, from my hungry childlike meddlings around the Mowgli kitchen. These fries are sweet, you don't need many, but there is something so wrong yet *so right* about them. And I bet they are the only Treacle Tamarind Fries on the planet.

4 large Maris Piper potatoes, cut into
   2cm/¾ inch cubes
½ tsp salt
¼ tsp ground turmeric
3 tbsp vegetable oil
100ml/3½fl oz/scant ½ cup Tamarind
   Treacle Sauce (see page 159)

1½ tsp chat masala
½ red onion, finely diced
1 small red chilli, finely sliced
½ bunch of fresh coriander/cilantro,
   roughly chopped

25

1 In a large saucepan set over a medium-high heat, add the chopped potatoes, salt and ground turmeric and cover with cold water. Bring up to the boil, then reduce the heat to low and simmer for 8–10 minutes or until the potatoes become soft but still hold together. Drain well and set aside.

2 In a large non-stick frying pan set over a medium-high heat, add the vegetable oil. When hot, add the drained potatoes and fry, stirring regularly, for 10 minutes or until the potatoes are golden and crisp.

3 Meanwhile, place a large non-stick frying pan over a medium-high heat, add the tamarind treacle sauce and reduce by about a half until sticky and gloopy. Toss the fried potatoes with the chat masala, then add to the tamarind treacle sauce and toss vigorously until fully coated. The potatoes should have a glossy sheen.

4 Finish by sprinkling over the red onion, red chilli and fresh coriander just before serving.

Pictured overleaf, left

FENUGREEK KISSED FRIES

PREP: 5 MINUTES • COOK: 20 MINUTES • SERVES 4–6

No Indian would fry potatoes without first rubbing them with turmeric. Turmeric is a deep, earthy flavoured root, ground to make a golden yellow powder. This spice adds to the earthiness of potatoes, which makes them taste sweeter and richer. I add fenugreek as it lifts them to another spicy level. This is how I cook my roast potatoes at home too, but with a sprinkling of brown sugar and garlic purée.

4 large Maris Piper potatoes, cut into
   2cm/¾ inch cubes
½ tsp salt
½ tsp ground turmeric
3 tbsp vegetable oil
½ tsp fenugreek seeds

½ red onion, finely sliced
1 small red chilli, finely sliced, plus
   extra to serve
½ bunch of fresh coriander/cilantro,
   roughly chopped, plus extra to serve
1 tbsp Green Chilli Pickle (see page 146)

1 In a large saucepan set over a medium-high heat, add the chopped potatoes, salt and ground turmeric and cover with cold water. Bring up to the boil, then reduce the heat to low and simmer for 8–10 minutes or until the potatoes become soft but still hold together. Drain well and set aside.

2 In a large non-stick frying pan set over a medium-high heat, add the vegetable oil. When hot, add the fenugreek and fry until the seeds turn a dark brown. Add the drained potatoes and fry, stirring regularly, for 10 minutes or until the potatoes are golden and crisp.

3 When cooked though, put the potatoes in a large bowl and toss with the red onion, red chilli, fresh coriander and green chilli pickle until everything is fully coated. Finish by garnishing with freshly sliced red chilli and fresh coriander just before serving.

Pictured on previous page, right

SPICED BROAD BEANS

Fried spiced legume snacks are beloved in India. Unlike potatoes, they can be dried in the heat of the sun and become long-life stalwarts. They are roasted and spiced and sold on every street corner. They are the home-from-school snack of a million Indian school children.

1kg/2lb 3oz bag frozen broad beans/
  fava beans
vegetable oil, for deep frying
1 tsp ground cumin

⅛ tsp paprika
½ tsp salt
½ tsp amchoor

1 Place the broad beans in a large bowl and cover with boiling water. After 8 minutes remove from the water and peel the beans by pressing the outer skin so the beans split into two.

2 Dry the peeled beans on paper towels.

3 Take a medium-size saucepan and set over a medium heat. Add enough vegetable oil until it is about 5cm/2 inches deep.

4 Heat the oil in the pan and deep-fry the beans until they are light brown. Remove and drain on paper towels. The beans become crispier as they cool.

5 Mix together the ground cumin, paprika, salt and amchoor, toss the drained beans in the mixture and serve.

29

YOGURT CHAT BOMBS

PREP: 25 MINUTES • COOK: 5 MINUTES • SERVES 2

Known in India as *dahi puri*, these are the ultimate flavour grenade and our biggest seller by far at Mowgli. They have their own Twitter following and fan club. Introducing someone to their first chat bomb became something of a cult culinary practice in Liverpool. They are the fiddliest things on earth and only last about 5 minutes before turning limp and falling apart, so Mowgli has a dedicated chat chef who makes each one to order and sends them straight out. The pani puri are the trickiest part of creating the chat bomb. The casing is made of simple ingredients, but the devil is in the detail. The dough has to be exactly the right density and needs to be dry enough to form a tight, waterproof fry. This is why Indians do not make these at home and instead street vendors become dedicated puri makers, making nothing else.

FOR THE TAMARIND WATER
45g/1½oz tamarind, seeds removed

FOR THE PANI PURI
80g/3oz/scant ½ cup fine semolina
80g/3oz/½ cup plain/all-purpose flour
3–4 tbsp soda water, more if needed
pinch of salt
vegetable oil, for deep frying

FOR THE FILLING
1 small red onion, finely diced
50g/2oz canned chickpeas/garbanzo
    beans, drained and rinsed
6 tsp Green Chilli Pickle (see page 146)
80g/3oz/¼ cup Cumin Raita (see
    page 160)
2 tbsp pomegranate seeds
2 tbsp fresh coriander/cilantro leaves
4 tbsp Sev Noodles (see page 135)

1 To make the tamarind water, place the tamarind into a bowl and pour over 250ml/9fl oz/1 cup boiling water. Leave to soak for 15 minutes. Using a fork mash the tamarind to a pulp, then strain the water into a clean bowl.

2 Pour 100ml/3½fl oz/scant ½ cup boiling water over the tamarind pulp and leave to soak for a further 15 minutes. Squeeze as much of the liquid as you can from the tamarind into the first batch of tamarind water. This makes more tamarind water than you need for this recipe but the extra can be stored in an airtight container in the refrigerator for up to 2 weeks.

3 In a large mixing bowl combine the semolina, flour, soda water and salt. Mix until it forms a stiff dough, then knead well for 5 minutes. Rest under a damp cloth for 15 minutes.

4 Take the dough and divide into 40 equal-size portions. Roll each portion into 4cm/1½ inch circles, as thin as you can, then place under a damp cloth and allow to rest for a further 5 minutes.

5 Take a large non-stick frying pan and set over a medium heat. Add enough vegetable oil until it is about 5cm/2 inches deep. To check the oil is ready for frying, take a little piece of dough and drop into the oil. It should sizzle, float to the top and turn a light brown.

6 When the oil is hot, carefully fry the pani puri in small batches for a couple of minutes. Give each puri a little press with a slotted spoon until they puff up and turn golden brown.

7 Remove from the oil and drain on paper towels. Once cool, any extra pani puri can be put in an airtight container and stored for up to 5 days.

8 Take six of the pani puri and break a hole in each one large enough to accommodate the filling ingredients.

9 Put 1 teaspoon of the chopped red onion into each pani puri, then add six chickpeas to each.

10 Next, fill each pani puri a third of the way up with the tamarind water, then add 1 teaspoon of the green chilli pickle and fill with the cumin raita.

11 Finish by dividing the pomegranate seeds between each pani puri, add a few fresh coriander leaves and a pinch of sev noodles. Serve straight away.

12 Eat in one bite!

Pictured overleaf, left

TAMARIND WATER BOMBS

PREP: 5 MINUTES • SERVES 2

I tried these on the Mowgli menu but they failed. I will resurrect them because they are the cornerstone of the Indian street stall scene. They are puri casings filled with a choice of different spiced waters. The eating of them therefore is very strange texturally. They are a crispy shell that explodes into a very uncompromising sharp, hot, zingy water. It was a bridge too far for my Mowgli clients 3 years ago. They will be back!

6 Pani Puri (see page 30–1)

FOR THE FILLING
1 red onion, finely diced
50g/2oz canned chickpeas/garbanzo
   beans, drained and rinsed

2 tbsp fresh mint, chopped
100ml/3½fl oz/scant ½ cup Tamarind
   Water (see page 30)
2 tbsp pomegranate seeds
2 tbsp fresh coriander/cilantro leaves
4 tbsp Sev Noodles (see page 135)

1 Break a hole in each pani puri large enough to accommodate the filling ingredients.

2 Put 1 teaspoon of the chopped red onion into each pani puri, then add six chickpeas to each and divide the fresh mint between them.

3 Next, fill each pani puri all the way up with the tamarind water.

4 Finish by dividing the pomegranate seeds between each pani puri, add a few fresh coriander leaves and a pinch of sev noodles. Serve straight away.

5 Eat in one bite!

Pictured on previous page, right

MOMOS
(NEPALESE STEAMED DUMPLINGS)

PREP: 30 MINUTES + 30 MINUTES CHILLING •
COOK: 15 MINUTES PER BATCH • MAKES 40 DUMPLINGS

These little Nepalese dumplings are all the rage in India. We are not a food culture that has much embraced the steamed dumpling, perhaps thanks to the texture. Our finger food tends to be crisp and fried, but enlightenment comes in the most surprising forms. This is now a common street snack across India. About time too.

500g/1lb 2oz/3⅓ cups plain/
   all-purpose flour
salt
1 litre/35fl oz/4¼ cups chicken stock
   or water, to fill steamer

FOR THE FILLING
400g/14oz pork belly, skin off
1 onion, roughly chopped
3–4 garlic cloves, chopped
3 sprigs of fresh coriander/
   cilantro, chopped
½ tsp salt

1 Put all the filling ingredients into a food processor, then blend to a medium paste. Chill for 30 minutes or so.

2 Meanwhile, put the flour and a pinch of salt in a bowl and add 6–9 tablespoons water gradually, mixing to form a stiff but pliable dough. Rest the dough for about 15–20 minutes, covered.

3 Roll the dough into 40 equal-size balls on a lightly floured surface. Individually, roll out each ball to a flat 5cm/2 inch circle. Put a generous teaspoon of filling in the centre and gather up the edges, crimping them together at the top, without leaving any flaps of dough, and using a little water to help them stick.

4 Add water or chicken stock to the bottom part of a steamer and bring up to the boil.

5 Arrange the dumplings in a lightly oiled steaming basket – you'll need to do this in batches – and steam over the simmering stock/water, covered, for about 12–15 minutes per batch. Serve straight away, in batches, or keep warm while you finish the remainder. Serve the dumplings warm with a chutney of your choice.

COURGETTE FLOWER BHAJIS

PREP: 10 MINUTES • COOK: 20 MINUTES • SERVES 4

Marrow and courgette/zucchini plants thrive in the warmth of the Indian sun and they are often found growing wild on rubbish heaps, so their flowers are not the rare treats they are in the West – they are common and fair game. They are also delicious. It has become almost de rigueur for chefs in the West to stuff them. We don't in India – we see the dense, spiced batter as a kind of outside stuffing. However this does not mean that you should not feel free to play around with stuffings too, if you want.

2 tbsp rice flour

200g/7oz/1⅔ cups gram/
    chickpea flour

½ tsp ground cumin

1 tsp ajwain seeds

2 tbsp chopped fresh coriander/cilantro

2 garlic cloves, crushed

1 tsp salt

½ tsp ground turmeric

⅛ tsp chilli powder

¼ tsp bicarbonate of soda/
    baking soda

sunflower oil, for deep frying

8 courgette/zucchini flowers

1 Combine the flours, cumin, ajwain seeds, coriander, garlic, salt, turmeric, chilli powder and bicarbonate of soda in a large mixing bowl and mix thoroughly. Add 300ml/10½fl oz/1¼ cups warm water and mix together to form a smooth, loose batter.

2 Heat the oil in a large wok over a high heat. Check the temperature has reached frying heat by dropping a touch of batter into the hot oil. It should bubble and float to the surface in a few seconds, golden brown, if the oil is at the right temperature.

3 Gently drop the courgette flowers two at a time into the batter, making sure they are fully coated.

4 Transfer the battered courgette flowers to the hot oil and cook for 2 minutes. Turn and fry for a further 2 minutes until they are evenly golden brown. Remove from the oil and drain on paper towels. Repeat in batches of two. Serve warm with a chutney of your choice.

MOWGLI ONION BHAJIS

PREP: 15 MINUTES • COOK: 20 MINUTES • MAKES 10–12 BHAJIS

These hot, flavourful treats take minutes to make and all they need is a starter onion... and we all have a starter onion lurking somewhere. Please also buy yourself a big bag of gram flour and forever change your snack life. This is a flour made of ground chickpeas/garbanzo beans, which makes it protein rich and gluten free. It can be used to make bhajis, deep-fried dumplings and pancakes – in fact wherever you have used flour in savoury dishes, just give gram flour a go. It feels heavier and less crisp than normal flour and the batter you create is very far from a western or tempura style, but in the heft, there is flavour and we Indians consider it an integral ingredient, not just a crispy shroud.

200g/7oz/1⅔ cups gram/
    chickpea flour
2 tbsp rice flour
½ tsp ground coriander
½ tsp ground cumin
¼ tsp ground turmeric
2 tbsp finely chopped fresh
    coriander/cilantro
2 garlic cloves, grated

2 green chillies, deseeded and
    finely chopped
1 tsp salt
1 tsp freshly ground black pepper
¼ tsp bicarbonate of soda/
    baking soda
1 tsp ajwain seeds
4 white onions, sliced into 1cm/
    ½ inch rings
vegetable oil, for deep frying

1 Combine all the ingredients except the onions and vegetable oil in a large bowl with 300ml/10½fl oz/1¼ cups warm water and mix thoroughly.

2 Set a large pan over a medium-high heat and fill a third of the way up with oil. You know the oil is hot enough when you can drop a small amount of batter into it and it bubbles and floats to the surface.

3 Toss a small batch of the onion rings into the batter, making sure they are fully coated. Carefully transfer the battered rings to the hot oil and fry for 2 minutes, then turn and fry for a further 3 minutes or until they are an even golden brown. Remove using a slotted spoon and drain well on paper towels. Repeat in small batches. Serve immediately.

BHEL PURI

PREP: 15 MINUTES • COOK: 2–3 MINUTES • SERVES 4–6

This tossed and tangy rice and nut rubble is sold outside every station, school and office in India. It is peddled in newspaper cones, often dry, with a little package of black salt to season. I struggled so much with trying to find an easy name for this on the menu. I'm still not content with names on the Mowgli menu that mean nothing to my English-speaking clients. I will get there. So far I have 'Tangy Rice Rubble' or, as someone once suggested, 'Spicy Cocoa Pops'? ... Nah.

250g/9oz puffed rice
75g/3oz finely diced red onion
100g/3½oz Sev Noodles (see page 135)
3 tbsp Coriander and Mint Chutney
   (see page 151)
3 tbsp Tamarind Chutney (see page 150)
2 tbsp Mowgli Chutney (see page 147)
1 large Maris Piper potato, peeled,
   boiled and chopped into 1cm/
   ½ inch cubes

1 green chilli, deseeded and
   finely sliced
½ small bunch of fresh coriander/
   cilantro, finely chopped
½ tsp chilli powder
1 tsp ground cumin
2 tsp chat masala
3 tbsp roasted peanuts
juice of ½ lemon
salt

1 In a large pan set over a high heat, dry roast the puffed rice until it is crispy, then set aside and allow to cool.

2 Once cooled, add all the other ingredients to the puffed rice in a large bowl and mix well. Season to taste and serve immediately.

40

2
STREET
MEATS

Meat on the street stalls of India can be a frightening thing. Remember that there is a general absence of refrigeration and so cold meats and cooked meats are not arrayed to sit and beckon customers. There are instead a number of factors that are important on the street meat stalls of the East.

Firstly, the marinade is critical. I know this is a pain, but it is so important that you get as many loud, aromatic spices in there as possible. This is really not a place for subtle spicings and restraint. The fish can take a lighter hand, but still you will see that I use the power of English mustard paste to do some of the tenderising legwork. Be brave and tweak these spicings to your taste. If you love cinnamon, add more in. In the Mowgli restaurants I keep chilli to a sane minimum, so do add more chilli powder if you are a heat junkie. This is the place that this kind of recklessness in rubs is entirely appropriate.

Strong marinades containing hugely aromatic garam masala spices along with pungent onion and garlic pastes all play a critical role in tenderising and, to some small extent, preserving the meat. The acids in these ingredients begin to break the meat down and prepare it for the power of the spices.

The aromatic acids within the spices can then penetrate and thoroughly perfume the meat and fish. Spices like cinnamon, cloves, cumin and cardamom all contain aromatic oils that help keep the meat smelling fresh and enticing as it softens in the marinade.

The cooking methods on these street stalls are typically fierce and uncompromising. The tandoor oven reaches extremely high heats that cook meat quickly and evenly. Charcoal grills are small and portable, and kick out a good heat for steaming fish in banana leaves.

Deep frying is the favourite mode of street food cooking. The oil plunge is the greatest safeguard against undercooked meat at the roadside kitchens. My mother would say all that is rank or dubious is burned away in the fizz of the oil. Not sure about that, but it is true that the bhaji is the baron of the pavement picnic.

GUNPOWDER CHICKEN

This dish was borne out of my fury when I paid through the nose for a teaspoon of popcorn chicken at a drive thru. My girls love popcorn chicken but I felt light in the pocket and light in the stomach. I went home and began to experiment with God's own batter – gram flour. These are a gluten-free, delicious bite. We use chicken breast in Mowgli, so this is the recipe I've given you here, but in India, the darker and bonier, the better, so use chicken thighs for a more tender, rich ammunition.

2 large chicken breasts, chopped into
    2cm/¾ inch pieces
2 tsp crushed garlic
1 tbsp ground cumin
1 tbsp ground coriander
2 tsp ground cinnamon
½ tsp salt
juice of ½ lemon
1 egg, beaten

380g/13½oz/generous 3 cups gram/
    chickpea flour
vegetable oil, for deep frying
1 large red chilli, finely sliced
½ red onion, finely sliced
1 tbsp chopped fresh coriander/cilantro
2 tbsp Tamarind Chutney (see page 150)
2 tbsp Green Chilli Pickle (see page 146)
¼ tsp salt

1 In a mixing bowl, toss the chicken pieces with the garlic, cumin, ground coriander, cinnamon, salt and lemon juice.

2 Add the beaten egg to the chicken and mix well. Take the chicken and toss in the gram flour, ensuring it is fully coated and knocking off the excess.

3 Heat a deep-fat fryer to 180°C/350°F or set a saucepan over a medium-high heat with about 4cm/1½ inches of oil. You know the oil is hot enough when you drop a small amount of batter into it and it floats to the surface. Fry the chicken in small batches for 6–8 minutes or until golden brown and cooked through. Carefully remove the chicken using a slotted spoon and drain on paper towels.

4 Once all the chicken has been fried, put in a large mixing bowl and toss with the red chilli, red onion, fresh coriander, tamarind chutney, green chilli pickle and salt. Serve immediately.

MOWGLI STICKY WINGS

PREP: 5 MINUTES + 3 HOURS MARINATING •
COOK: 45 MINUTES • SERVES 4–6

Having crispy, sweet, sticky, meat-smothered finger food is important to me for the sake of my soul and my hips. I could not have a restaurant that was not able to be all things to all people, and all people need to get their hands dirty with something that sits in the intersection between dessert and dinner. I wanted a rich, fruity, dark treacle finish for these wings. Date syrup does the fruity and black treacle/molasses brings the rich darkness.

4 tbsp date syrup

2 tbsp black treacle/molasses

3 garlic cloves, minced

5cm/2 inch piece of fresh root ginger, peeled and grated

1 tsp garam masala

2 tsp ground cumin

½ tsp black mustard seeds

4 teaspoons dark rum

juice of ½ lemon

2 tbsp white wine vinegar

1 tsp salt

1kg/2lb 3oz chicken wings

48

1 In a large bowl, add all the ingredients except for the chicken wings and mix well. Add the chicken wings, then cover and refrigerate for at least 3 hours.

2 Preheat your oven to 200°C/400°F/gas 6. Spread the wings out in an even layer on a large roasting pan and roast in the oven for 40–45 minutes, turning once, until cooked through, golden and sticky. Remove from the oven and serve immediately.

ANGRY ROAST CHICKEN

PREP: 5 MINUTES + 4 HOURS MARINATING •
COOK: 1½ HOURS • SERVES 4

I loved this Mowgli dish. It was a succulent whole roast chicken with the Angry Bird tandoori spices applied and roasted to a royal red splendour. We used to serve it on a large platter surrounded by fenugreek fries with a knife stuck into its crown. It was a delicious, dramatic, sharing dish. This is something we still wheel out for special group occasions.

1 whole chicken, about 1.6kg/3½lb

3 tbsp vegetable oil

Fenugreek Kissed Fries, to serve
   (see page 28)

Rotis, to serve (see page 130)

FOR THE SPICE RUB

300g/10½oz/generous 1 cup
   plain yogurt

½ tsp ground turmeric

½ tsp chilli powder

2 tsp ground coriander

1½ tsp ground cumin

½ tsp ground cinnamon

½ tsp ground cloves

3 garlic cloves, minced

7.5cm/3 inch piece of fresh root
   ginger, peeled and grated

juice of ½ lemon

1½ tsp salt

1 In a large bowl combine all the spice rub ingredients and mix well until everything is fully combined.

2 Take the chicken and cut three deep gashes in each breast and two diagonal gashes in each thigh. Put the chicken in a bowl, take the spice rub and spread it all over the chicken, ensuring the mix gets into all the gashes. Cover and refrigerate for at least 4 hours, preferably overnight.

3 Preheat the oven to 200°C/400°F/gas 6. Take the chicken out of the refrigerator 30 minutes before you plan to cook it, allowing it to come up to room temperature. Place the chicken in a large roasting pan and drizzle with the vegetable oil, then roast for 1 hour 20 minutes, basting the chicken halfway through cooking, until cooked through and tender. Serve immediately with the fenugreek kissed fries and rotis.

Pictured overleaf

ANGRY BIRD

PREP: 5 MINUTES + 4 HOURS MARINATING •
COOK: 40 MINUTES • SERVES 4

Thighs or drumsticks are the best meats for this simple tandoori dish, though this is a great marinade for any meats or fish that you can then roast, grill/broil or barbecue. The yogurt and lemon go a long way in helping to tenderise the meat and almost break down the structure so that the spices can better penetrate. Use mild paprika powder to give a good flavour and colour. In India they use chilli powder, which makes this dish seriously hot.

8 skin-on, bone-in chicken thighs

FOR THE MARINADE
500g/1lb 2oz/2 cups plain yogurt
½ tsp ground turmeric
½ tsp chilli powder
1 large green chilli, deseeded and
    finely sliced
2 tsp ground cumin

2 tsp ground coriander
1 tsp ground cinnamon
2 tbsp paprika
½ tsp ground cloves
5cm/2 inch piece of fresh root ginger,
    peeled and grated
3 garlic cloves, minced
½ tsp salt
juice of ½ lemon

1 In a mixing bowl large enough to hold the chicken thighs, add all the ingredients for the marinade and mix well until everything is fully combined. Add the chicken thighs, cover and refrigerate for at least 4 hours, preferably overnight.

2 Preheat the oven to 220°C/430°F/gas 7. Remove the chicken thighs from the marinade and wipe off any excess, then lay in a single layer on a roasting pan and roast for 35–40 minutes or until the chicken is golden, cooked through and tender. Remove from the oven and serve immediately.

52

MAA'S LAMB CHOPS

PREP: 5 MINUTES + 4 HOURS MARINATING •
COOK: 10 MINUTES • SERVES 4

This dish makes us no money. The margins are awful and the chops are a pain because they snarl up the chefs and the grill, but they are the taste of parties at my mother's house. This is, more than anything, the dish that conjures up the smell in Mowgli. When I walk into Mowgli every day, the aroma takes me straight to the excitement of a party night in Skelmersdale in the 1970s. This is the dish that me and my children eat most often in Mowgli. So margins can go to hell. This is Mowgli home from home for us.

8 lamb chops, about 2.5cm/
   1 inch thick
500g/1lb 2oz/2 cups plain yogurt
2 tbsp ground cumin
2 tbsp paprika
1 tsp ground cloves
1 tsp ground green cardamom
1 tsp fenugreek powder

1 tsp ground turmeric
juice of 1 lemon
4 garlic cloves, minced
1 tbsp minced fresh root ginger
2 tsp salt
Mowgli Slaw, to serve (see page 140)
Carrot Salad, to serve (see page 140)
Rotis, to serve (see page 130)

1 In a bowl large enough to hold the lamb chops, mix the yogurt, cumin, paprika, cloves, cardamom, fenugreek, turmeric, lemon juice, garlic, ginger and salt, then add the lamb chops and massage the marinade into them, making sure they are fully covered. Cover and leave to marinate in the refrigerator for at least 4 hours, preferably overnight.

2 Preheat the grill/broiler to its highest setting. Put the chops on a baking sheet and grill/broil for 3–4 minutes on each side for a medium-rare chop.

3 Serve with the Mowgli slaw, carrot salad and fresh rotis.

TAMARIND TREACLE RIBS

PREP: 15 MINUTES • COOK: 2½ HOURS • SERVES 4

This was such a well-loved dish in Mowgli, but I cannot have an infinite menu. I felt that the Mowgli Sticky Wings (see page 48) covered that intersection between dessert, dinner and finger food, so having two dishes achieving the same experiential end was a waste of an opportunity to introduce a new and weird dish to our clients. It was only for this reason that I took it off the menu for a while. I cook it at home all the time and get asked about it every day in the restaurant, but I must be strong.

1.5kg/3lb 5oz pork spare ribs

1 tsp salt

2 star anise

3 green cardamom pods

1½ tsp ground cumin

2 tbsp black treacle/molasses

3 garlic cloves, peeled

2.5cm/1 inch piece of fresh root
    ginger, peeled

1 green chilli, finely sliced

125g/4oz/⅔ cup soft brown sugar

1 tbsp tamarind concentrate

1 Place the ribs in a large saucepan set over a medium-high heat, add the salt and cover with water (about 3 litres/105fl oz/13 cups or more depending on the size of the ribs). Add the star anise, green cardamom pods, ground cumin, black treacle, garlic, ginger and green chilli and bring up to the boil. Once boiling, reduce the heat to low and cover with a lid. Simmer gently for 1–1½ hours or until the ribs are tender. Remove the ribs from the liquor and set aside.

2 With the pan still on the heat, add the brown sugar and tamarind concentrate and carefully reduce the cooking liquor until there is about 2cm/¾ inch left in the bottom of the pan – it should be thick and glossy. Remove from the heat and allow to cool, then blend in a food processor until smooth.

3 Preheat your oven to 220°C/430°F/gas 7. Place the ribs on a baking sheet, then cover with the tamarind glaze. Roast in the oven for 20–25 minutes, basting regularly with the glaze, until blackened, cooked through and tender. Serve immediately.

BENGALI WHITEBAIT BITES

PREP: 15 MINUTES + 1 HOUR CHILLING •
COOK: 10 MINUTES PER BATCH • SERVES 4

Goodness, Bengalis love whitebait. We are the ultimate fish lovers and this dish has the wonderful accessibility of also being perfect finger food. On the streets of India we buy these in generous paper cones and walk along, knocking them back with gay abandon. I had whitebait served similarly in Seville, a gorgeous crunch but I did miss the spice.

400g/14oz whitebait

juice of 1 lime

1 tsp ground turmeric

2 tsp chilli powder

1 tsp ground cumin

1cm/½ inch piece of fresh root ginger, peeled and roughly chopped

3 garlic cloves, roughly chopped

50g/2oz/⅓ cup plain/all-purpose flour

50g/2oz/scant ½ cup gram/chickpea flour

1 tbsp rice flour

salt

4 tbsp vegetable oil

1 Wash and drain the whitebait well and place in a dish. Rub with the lime juice and then the turmeric, chilli and cumin. Leave covered in the refrigerator for at least 1 hour.

2 Grind the ginger and garlic to a paste in a mortar. Mix the three flours with the paste and add salt to taste. Toss the fish in this dry coating.

3 Heat the oil in a heavy wok-style pan and fry the fish in batches over a medium heat until crisp. This should take about 8–10 minutes each time. Drain well and serve hot.

FISH PAKORAS

PREP: 15 MINUTES + 1 HOUR MARINATING •
COOK: 15 MINUTES • SERVES 4

Pakora is just another word for bhaji – another excuse for that gram flour batter. This is as close as Indians get to fish fingers. Play with the batter to make this a bespoke favourite. Lime zest and your choice of herbs finely chopped are a good twist.

450g/1lb skinned white fish fillets, such as cod or haddock, chopped into 2.5cm/1 inch chunks

vegetable oil, for deep frying

fresh coriander/cilantro

FOR THE MARINADE

1 tbsp lemon juice

3 garlic cloves, minced

2.5cm/1 inch piece of fresh root ginger, peeled and grated

¼ tsp ground turmeric

½ tsp salt

½ tsp ground cumin

FOR THE BATTER

200g/7oz/1⅔ cups gram/ chickpea flour

½ tsp bicarbonate of soda/ baking soda

½ tsp salt

¼ tsp chilli powder

¼ tsp ground turmeric

½ tsp garam masala

1 Mix the fish with the marinade ingredients, cover and set aside in the refrigerator for at least an hour.

2 Mix together the ingredients for the batter. Slowly pour 275–300ml/10–10½fl oz/ 1–1¼ cups water into the dry ingredients and mix well – you want it to form a smooth paste.

3 Heat a deep-fat fryer to 180°C/350°F or set a saucepan over a medium-high heat with about 4cm/1½ inches of oil. You know the oil is hot enough when you drop a small amount of batter into it and it floats to the surface.

4 Coat the fish pieces in the batter and carefully fry in small batches for 3–5 minutes until they are golden brown and cooked through. Remove from the oil using a slotted spoon and drain thoroughly on paper towels.

5 Finish with fresh coriander and serve immediately.

INDIAN FISH AND CHIPS

PREP: 10 MINUTES • COOK: 25 MINUTES • SERVES 4–6

This is an awesome adaptation of a British classic. Indian chips have a typically deep golden, come-hither look. The batter is a gluten-free gram batter and, remember, it is heavier and slightly softer than a Western batter, so don't expect the brusque bite.

4 large Maris Piper potatoes, peeled
   and sliced into chunky chips
1 tbsp plus ½ tsp ground turmeric
1 tbsp sea salt
120g/4oz/1 cup gram/chickpea flour,
   plus extra to sprinkle
½ tsp salt

1 tsp baking powder
⅛ tsp chilli powder
4 white fish fillets, such as cod
   or haddock
lemon wedges, to serve
Mowgli Chutney (see page 147),
   to serve

1 Bring a large saucepan of salted water up to the boil, reduce the heat to low and completely submerge your chips, simmering for 8–10 minutes until they start to soften around the edges but are still firm. Drain in a colander and sprinkle over the tablespoon of ground turmeric and the salt. Give the potatoes a good shake to make sure they are covered in the turmeric.

2 While the potatoes are boiling, make your batter. Sift the gram flour into a mixing bowl with the salt, baking powder, ½ teaspoon of ground turmeric and the chilli powder and mix, then slowly start to pour in 200ml/7fl oz/scant 1 cup water, whisking all the while. You're looking for a thick batter consistency.

3 Heat a deep-fat fryer to 180°C/350°F or set a saucepan over a medium-high heat with about 4cm/1½ inches of oil. You know the oil is hot enough when you drop a small amount of batter into it and it floats to the surface. Using a large metal slotted spoon, carefully submerge the chips in the oil and cook for 8–10 minutes until golden and crispy. Once cooked, remove gently and place on paper towels to drain, then set aside.

4 Sprinkle the fish with a little gram flour, then dip into the batter and shake off any excess. Carefully lower each piece of fish into the deep-fat fryer and fry for around 4 minutes or until golden and crispy.

5 Serve immediately with lemon wedges and Mowgli chutney.

SPICED BUTTERFLY PRAWNS

PREP: 20 MINUTES + 30 MINUTES MARINATING
• COOK: 20 MINUTES • SERVES 4

These prawns make great finger food starters. The marinade is all important as it is what takes them from buffet to banquet. The short fry means they stay moist and full of explosive flavour.

4 king prawns/jumbo shrimp, about 200g/7oz in total, or 8 medium prawns/shrimp, about 100g/3½oz in total

175g/6oz dried breadcrumbs

vegetable oil, for shallow frying

1 lemon, cut into wedges, to serve

FOR THE MARINADE

1 small onion, roughly chopped

3 garlic cloves, roughly chopped

1cm/½ inch piece of fresh root ginger, peeled and roughly chopped

2 green chillies, roughly chopped

½ tsp garam masala

¼ tsp freshly ground black pepper

½ tsp ground turmeric

juice of ½ lemon

pinch of sugar

1 Shell the prawns and remove the heads, leaving the tails on. Devein the prawns by slicing all the way down the back, but not through, then open them out and wash out the black intestine. Open the prawns out further by slicing into each side of the flesh and unfolding them outwards to make large ovals with the tail at one end. Put the prawns in a dish.

2 In a food processor, blend the onion, garlic, ginger and chillies together to make a fine paste, then mix with the remaining marinade ingredients. Rub this paste on all sides of the butterflied prawns and leave to marinate for about 30 minutes.

3 Put the breadcrumbs on a flat plate. Heat the oil in a frying pan over a medium heat. Dip the prawns into the breadcrumbs and press down to coat well on both sides.

4 Fry the prawns individually at first. Put one prawn in the oil, and hold it down with a flat spoon to prevent it curling. Cook for about 1½ minutes, then turn and cook for another 1½ minutes. Once the prawn has been turned it will not curl up, so you can add the next one. Proceed in this way until all the prawns are cooked.

5 Drain on absorbent paper towels and serve with a chutney of your choice.

BARBECUE BENGALI MACKEREL

This fish dish is perfect for foil tents on the barbecue and equally brilliant in the oven for a quick supper. This is how Indians would barbecue their fish if barbecues were a big thing over there. English mustard, coriander/cilantro and green chilli are a Bengali trio made in heaven and really give any fish a fragrant punch.

4 small whole mackerel, 500g/1lb 2oz each, scaled and gutted

3 tbsp vegetable oil

1 tbsp English mustard paste

3 large green chillies, deseeded and finely sliced

1 bunch of fresh coriander/cilantro, leaves roughly chopped, stalks kept

1 tsp ground turmeric

juice of 2 limes

1 tsp salt

Puris (see page 134) or rice to serve

1 Preheat your barbecue or preheat your oven to 220°C/430°F/gas 7.

2 Score the mackerel on both sides, then rub the vegetable oil, mustard paste, green chilli, coriander leaves, turmeric, lime juice and salt into the fish. Stuff the belly cavities of the fish with the squeezed limes and coriander stalks.

3 Wrap foil loosely around each fish to form a tented package.

4 Barbecue the fish or roast in the oven for 10–12 minutes. Remove the fish from the foil parcels and serve with either rice or puris.

65

3

THE HINDU KITCHEN

My passion for Indian cooking stems from the clever and simple flavour creation in the vegetarian dishes. In food shacks in India the majority of the menu is great vegan and vegetarian fare, while the minority eating pursuit is the meat section, often given the ignominious menu heading 'Non-Veg Dishes'. Hilarious and wonderful. Indians rank their meat dishes as second-rate cousins, overshadowed by the absence of vegetables. How different the emphasis is on the menus across Britain.

For Mowgli I never wanted that apology of a lower-case '(v)' after vegetarian and vegan dishes. No, these are the dishes that are most precious to me. These are the dishes that I eat every day in my home, as did my ancestors. I was tempted to employ the 'Non-Veg' phrasing for meat dishes, but it felt a bit churlish. So the titles 'Hindu Kitchen' and 'Street Meats' demarcate my dishes and leave both with the dignity they deserve.

My family are Hindu Brahmins and my father was a priest. Hinduism has an almost medicolegal relationship with food. Various ingredients are forbidden at certain times and many Hindus fast as greedily as they eat. In this relationship of 'Thou shalt not,' there is a pressure on home cooks to produce virtuosity without the usual big-hitting flavour givers. Often onion, garlic, meat and eggs are forbidden. The strength and genius of the Hindu kitchen, then, lies in the vegan dishes that are produced with just a few alchemical touches.

68

Remember that the headnote spices for vegetables tend to be the seed spices such as cumin, nigella, mustard seed and panch phoron. These seed spices, when fried in a touch of oil, release layer upon layer of scents and aromatic oils. It is the leaching of these aromatic oils into the cooking oils that almost 'dresses' the delicate vegetables and encourages out of them hidden and myriad flavours.

There are two critical points that I insist my chefs understand before even approaching a Mowgli pan. The first is that the starting moment of any of the dishes in the Hindu kitchen is a sacred one that involves the whole attention of the chef, a good slug of hot oil and time to fry the spices until they have fully frizzled and browned. Only then can one move on to the next stage. I describe these dormant seed spices as akin to expensive scented candles. It is only when they are set alight that they release their true flavours and full potential. Nothing else must go into that pan until the seeds are all done with their awakening.

The second, critical point is that tomatoes, when added to vegetable dishes, must be given time and patience to cook from acidic red, to caramelised, warm brown. The chemistry in the pan involves those aromatic oils percolating up through the waters of the tomato, intensifying the sugars as they barge through and turning tartness to tang.

69

ALOO GHOBI

PREP: 5 MINUTES • COOK: 30 MINUTES • SERVES 4

This is the ultimate barometer of the skill of an Indian home cook. It is the most basic of dishes, just cauli and potato, so what could go wrong! Lots. This is a dish that is all about patience and a low, slow cook. This is the ultimate test in the subtlety of spicing. Overspice and you kill the cauli, underspice and you have hospital food.

4 tbsp vegetable oil

1 tsp cumin seeds

1 large green chilli, pierced

1 large potato, peeled and cut into
    2cm/¾ inch chunks

1 large cauliflower, cut into florets

¼ tsp ground turmeric

1 tsp ground coriander

¼ tsp English mustard paste

⅛ tsp chilli powder

1 tsp salt

1 tsp sugar

1 Put the oil in a large heavy saucepan set over a medium-high heat. When hot, add the cumin seeds and green chilli and fry until the cumin seeds turn a deep golden brown and become fragrant. Turn the heat down to low and add the cubed potato, then cook gently for 8 minutes until it starts to soften at the edges.

2 Add the cauliflower florets, ground turmeric, ground coriander, mustard paste, chilli powder, salt and sugar and give everything a good mix together until the cauliflower is fully coated with the spices.

3 Cover with a lid and cook gently for 15–20 minutes, adding a splash of water if necessary and stirring occasionally, until the cauliflower is tender and cooked through.

TEA-STEEPED CHICKPEAS

Chole bhature is one of India's most common street food dishes. The chole are the curried chickpeas/garbanzo beans that have a typical tang lent to them by tea leaves. The tannins in the tea are central to giving a sharp edge to this rich dish. The bhatura is a soft fried bread. At Mowgli, this vegan dish is extremely poplular and it works brilliantly with our puri breads on page 134.

4 tbsp vegetable oil

1½ tsp cumin seeds

2 bay leaves

2 small white onions, finely diced

5cm/2 inch piece of fresh root ginger, peeled and grated

3 garlic cloves, minced

2 tsp ground cumin

2 tsp ground coriander

2 tsp ground cloves

1 tsp ground cinnamon

½ tsp chilli powder

¼ tsp ground turmeric

400g/14oz canned chopped tomatoes

2 x 400g/14oz cans chickpeas/ garbanzo beans, drained and rinsed

4 tbsp strong breakfast tea

1 tsp salt

1 tsp caster/granulated sugar

200g/7oz spinach, washed and roughly chopped

1 small bunch of fresh coriander/ cilantro, roughly chopped

1 Put the vegetable oil in a large heavy saucepan set over a medium-high heat. When hot, add the cumin seeds and fry until they turn dark brown and fragrant, then turn the heat down to medium and add the bay leaves, onions, ginger and garlic and fry for 8 minutes until the onions are soft and dark brown.

2 Add the ground cumin, coriander, cloves and cinnamon and cook for 2 minutes, then add the chilli powder, ground turmeric, tomatoes, chickpeas, tea, salt and sugar and simmer gently for 20–25 minutes until thick and tangy.

3 Finish by stirring through the chopped spinach leaves and coriander just before serving.

TEMPLE DAHL

PREP: 10 MINUTES • COOK: 30 MINUTES • SERVES 4–6

The purest item on the Mowgli menu. This has no onion or garlic and is the simplest and most digestible of Indian dishes. It is given to infants, invalids and priests during their most prayerful ceremonies. Remember, Hindu custom suggests that the tainting qualities of onion and garlic are forbidden. Well, this dahl is the epitome of everything that is right.

250g/9oz red lentils
200g/7oz canned chopped tomatoes
¼ tsp ground turmeric
3 tbsp vegetable oil or 1 tbsp ghee
1 tsp cumin seeds
1 small green chilli, pierced
1 tsp caster/granulated sugar

1½ tsp salt
¼ tsp chilli powder
juice of ½ lemon
1 small bunch of fresh coriander/
    cilantro, leaves and stalks
    finely chopped

1 In a medium-size saucepan add the lentils, chopped tomatoes and turmeric, then cover with 1 litre/35fl oz/4¼ cups water and stir together. Bring up to the boil, then reduce the heat to low, cover with a lid and simmer gently for 18–20 minutes, stirring occasionally and adding more water if necessary, until the lentils are tender. Remove from the heat and set aside.

2 Put the vegetable oil (or ghee if using) in a large non-stick frying pan set over a medium-high heat. When hot, add the cumin seeds and green chilli and fry for 30 seconds.

3 Turn the heat down to medium. Take the lentils and carefully ladle them into the frying pan, stirring until everything is mixed. Bring up to the boil and add the sugar, salt, chilli powder and lemon juice, then remove from the heat.

4 Add a splash more water to loosen if necessary – the dahl should have the consistency of porridge or can be loosened with water to taste. Finish by stirring in the chopped coriander just before serving.

GREEN DAHL
WITH RHUBARB AND GINGER

PREP: 10 MINUTES • COOK: 1½ HOURS • SERVES 4–6

My grandmother used to love sour dahls. In India she used raw green mango to run a refreshing sourness under her pulses. When she came to the UK, she toyed with unripe plums, but settled for the tart charm of rhubarb.

250g/9oz green mung beans

200g/7oz canned chopped tomatoes

¼ tsp ground turmeric

¼ tsp chilli powder

5 tbsp vegetable oil

1½ tsp cumin seeds

½ tsp mustard seeds

1 large green chilli, pierced

2 bay leaves

2 white onions, thinly sliced

8cm/3 inch piece of fresh root ginger, peeled and grated

3 garlic cloves, grated

250g/9oz fresh rhubarb, chopped into 5cm/2 inch pieces

juice of ½ lemon

1 tsp salt

1 tsp sugar

1 small bunch of fresh coriander/ cilantro, roughly chopped

1 In a medium-size saucepan add the green mung beans, 1 litre/35fl oz/4¼ cups water, chopped tomatoes, turmeric and chilli powder, then bring up to the boil. Reduce the heat to low and simmer gently for 50–60 minutes or until the beans are soft and tender, adding more water if needed, then set aside.

2 Put the vegetable oil in a large non-stick frying pan and set over a medium-high heat. When hot, add the cumin and mustard seeds and fry until they turn dark brown, then add the green chilli, bay leaves, white onions, ginger and garlic and fry for 8 minutes or until the onions are soft and golden.

3 Turn the heat down to medium, then take the beans and carefully ladle them into the pan with the onions, add the chopped rhubarb, lemon juice, salt and sugar and bring up to the boil. Reduce the heat to low and simmer gently for 6 minutes or until the rhubarb is cooked through and tender. Finish by stirring though the fresh coriander. Add a splash more water to loosen if necessary – the dahl should have the consistency of thick porridge.

Pictured overleaf: Temple Dahl, far left; Green Dahl, second left

BLACK DAHL

PREP: 10 MINUTES • COOK: 2 HOURS • SERVES 4–6

This is the staple dahl for many Indians – wonderfully filling and fabulously vegan. With big hitting flavours, this is one of those dishes that makes veganism easy.

250g/9oz urid dahl

400g/14oz canned chopped tomatoes

¼ tsp ground turmeric

2 tbsp vegetable oil

1½ tsp cumin seeds

2 large green chillies, deseeded and
  thinly sliced

2 bay leaves

2 small white onions, thinly sliced

8cm/3 inch piece of fresh root ginger,
  peeled and grated

5 garlic cloves, minced

3 tsp ground cumin

2 tsp ground coriander

½ tsp ground cloves

½ tsp ground cardamom

1¼ tsp ground cinnamon

¼ tsp ground nutmeg

¼ tsp chilli powder

juice of ½ lemon

1 tsp salt

1 tsp sugar

½ small bunch of fresh coriander/
  cilantro, leaves and stalks chopped

1 In a medium-size saucepan add the urid dahl, chopped tomatoes and turmeric, then cover with 1.5 litres/52fl oz/6½ cups cold water and stir together. Bring up to the boil, then reduce the heat to low, cover and simmer for 1½–1¾ hours or until the lentils are tender and cooked through. Remove from the heat and set aside.

2 Put the vegetable oil in a large non-stick frying pan set over a medium-high heat. When hot, add the cumin seeds and fry until they turn dark brown. Add the green chilli and bay leaves and fry for a further 20 seconds. Add the onions, ginger and garlic and fry for 6 minutes or until they soften and turn golden brown.

3 Add the ground cumin, coriander, cloves, cardamom, cinnamon, nutmeg and chilli powder and fry for 30 seconds. Carefully ladle the cooked lentils into the pan with the spices and onions and stir until everything is fully mixed.

4 Bring the lentils up to the boil, adding more water if necessary, then stir through the lemon juice, salt and sugar. The dahl should have the consistency of thick porridge. Finish by stirring through the chopped fresh coriander.

Pictured on previous page: Black Dahl, second right; Red Lentil and Spinach Dahl, far right

RED LENTIL AND SPINACH DAHL

PREP: 10 MINUTES • COOK: 35 MINUTES • SERVES 4–6

I dreamt of opening a Mowgli that served only dahls and rice. There are so many wonderful things you can do with lentils and all of them are so different yet leave you feeling full, but healthily so. Any dahl works wonderfully with spinach tossed in towards the end. It's a great way to get health by stealth into your loved ones.

250g/9oz red lentils
200g/7oz canned chopped tomatoes
¼ tsp ground turmeric
3 tbsp vegetable oil
2 tsp cumin seeds
½ tsp asafoetida
1 tsp mustard seeds
1 large green chilli, pierced

¼ tsp chilli powder
250g/9oz spinach, washed
1 tsp caster/granulated sugar
2 tsp salt
juice of ½ lemon
1 small bunch of fresh coriander/
    cilantro, leaves and stalks
    finely chopped

1 In a medium-size saucepan add the lentils, chopped tomatoes and turmeric, then cover with 750ml/26fl oz/3¼ cups cold water and stir together. Bring up to the boil, then reduce the heat to low, cover and simmer gently for 25–30 minutes, stirring occasionally and adding more water if necessary, until the lentils are tender. Remove from the heat and set aside.

2 Put the vegetable oil in a large non-stick frying pan set over a medium-high heat. When hot, add the cumin seeds, asafoetida, mustard seeds, green chilli and chilli powder and fry for 30 seconds until the seeds become brown and fragrant.

3 Turn the heat down to medium, then take the lentils and carefully ladle them into the pan with the cumin seeds. Add the fresh spinach and stir until everything is fully mixed. Bring up to the boil and add the sugar, salt and lemon juice, then remove from the heat.

4 Add a splash more water to loosen if necessary – the dahl should have the consistency of thick porridge. Finish by stirring in the chopped coriander just before serving.

PICNIC POTATO CURRY

PREP: 5 MINUTES • COOK: 50 MINUTES • SERVES 4

Indians love picnics. They choose spicings and ingredients that taste better when they are eaten cold. In Mowgli, we use potatoes alone in this dish, but at home very often we add a few chopped radishes into the cook – radishes and potatoes are a beloved ingredient combination. This gives a different texture and a tender, zesty surprise.

5 tbsp vegetable oil

1 large dried red chilli, pierced

½ tsp cumin seeds

½ tsp fennel seeds

¼ tsp fenugreek seeds

⅛ tsp black mustard seeds

2 small white onions, cut in half then thinly sliced lengthways

2 large Maris Piper potatoes, peeled and chopped into 2cm/¾ inch cubes

¼ tsp ground turmeric

¼ tsp chilli powder

200g/7oz radishes, halved

200g/7oz canned chopped tomatoes

1 tsp salt

1 tsp caster/granulated sugar

1 tbsp English mustard, loosened with a little water

1 Put the vegetable oil in a large non-stick frying pan set over a medium-high heat. When hot, add the dried red chilli and seed spices and cook for 30 seconds until the nuggets of fenugreek turn a golden brown and the mustard seeds turn grey. Lower the heat to medium, add the sliced onions and fry for 8 minutes until they turn a deep golden brown.

2 Turn the heat down to low, add the potatoes, ground turmeric, chilli powder, radishes and chopped tomatoes and stir until everything is fully mixed with the onions. Partially cover and cook gently for 30 minutes, stirring occasionally, until the potatoes are soft and cooked through. Remove the lid and continue to cook for a further 5 minutes until the oil has started to separate out from the tomatoes.

3 To finish, add the salt, sugar and the watered down English mustard and mix well.

KOHLRABI AND GINGER CURRY

Fenugreek and asafoetida are the ultimate invigorating spices. They are the nuclear weapons in the Indian kitchen and transform humble, lacklustre ingredients into something sublime. Invest in these spices and experiment with the humblest vegetables you can find – courgette/zucchini, potatoes or turnips all benefit from this spice makeover.

4 tbsp vegetable oil
1 tsp fenugreek seeds
¼ tsp asafoetida
1 kohlrabi, finely sliced
¼ tsp ground turmeric
⅛ tsp chilli powder

1 tsp salt
1 tsp caster/granulated sugar
1 tbsp garam masala
5cm/2 inch piece of fresh root ginger, peeled and grated
juice of ½ lemon

82

1 Put the vegetable oil in a large non-stick frying pan set over a medium-high heat. When hot, add the fenugreek seeds and, being careful not to burn them, fry until they turn fragrant and dark brown. Quickly add the asafoetida and fry for a further 10 seconds until it releases its pungent aroma.

2 Add the sliced kohlrabi, 800ml/28fl oz/scant 3½ cups water, ground turmeric, chilli powder, salt and sugar and stir until everything is mixed, then partially cover and cook gently on a low heat for 25 minutes or until the kohlrabi is tender.

3 When the kohlrabi is cooked through, add the garam masala and grated ginger, then continue to cook for a further 5 minutes. Finish with the fresh lemon juice. Add more water if necessary to loosen to your taste.

BENGALI ROOT VEG MEDLEY

White poppy seeds are a common ingredient in India that we use to give tame vegetables an oomph. They are best ground and then fried. I sometimes toss them through squash and root vegetable dishes for a nutty crunch.

80ml/2½fl oz/⅓ cup vegetable oil

1 tsp nigella seeds

2 large green chillies, deseeded and thinly sliced

1 small white onion, halved and thinly sliced

2 large Maris Piper potatoes, peeled and chopped into 2cm/¾ inch cubes

1 parsnip, peeled and chopped into 2cm/¾ inch cubes

2 carrots, peeled and chopped into 2cm/¾ inch cubes

¼ tsp ground turmeric

⅛ tsp chilli powder

1½ tsp salt

80g/3oz/½ cup garden peas

2 tbsp white poppy seeds

1 small bunch of fresh coriander/cilantro, leaves and stalks roughly chopped

1 Put 60ml/2fl oz/¼ cup of the vegetable oil in a large non-stick frying pan over a medium-high heat. When hot, add the nigella seeds and fry until they start to crackle and become fragrant. Lower the heat to medium, add the green chilli and onions and fry for 8 minutes until the onions soften and turn golden brown.

2 Turn the heat down to low and add the potatoes, parsnip, carrots, ground turmeric, chilli powder and 1 teaspoon of the salt and stir to mix with the onions. Partially cover and cook gently for 25–30 minutes, stirring occasionally, until the vegetables are completely soft and cooked through. Remove the lid, add the peas and cook for a further 5 minutes until the potatoes and parnsips have crisped up a little.

3 Grind the white poppy seeds in a pestle and mortar until they turn into a paste, then, in a separate medium-size saucepan, add the remaining vegetable oil and set over a high heat. When hot, add the white poppy seeds and fry for 20 seconds, taking care not to burn them, until they turn a light brown.

4 Once the potatoes are cooked through and tender, stir the browned poppy seeds through the potatoes, then season with the remaining salt and finish with the fresh coriander just before serving.

CALCUTTA TANGLED GREENS

This dish is at the heart of everything Mowgli is about. It is a dish that we eat at home at least twice a week. It is the best that Indians can do with the best of the humble, overwintered, robust, chlorophyll-rich, Great British veg.

3 tbsp vegetable oil

1 tbsp mustard seeds

2 garlic cloves, minced

2.5cm/1 inch piece of fresh root
    ginger, peeled and grated

1 white cabbage, quartered, cored and
    finely shredded

½ tsp ground turmeric

¼ tsp chilli powder

1 tsp salt

1 tsp caster/granulated sugar

1 tsp English mustard, loosened
    with a little water

juice of ½ lemon

1   Put the vegetable oil in a large non-stick frying pan set over a medium heat. When hot, add the mustard seeds and fry until they fizz and pop. Add the garlic and ginger and continue to fry for 30 seconds, taking care not to burn the garlic.

2   Add the white cabbage, ground turmeric, chilli powder, salt, sugar and English mustard and mix well, then cover with a lid and cook, stirring occasionally, for 25–30 minutes or until the cabbage is cooked through and tender.

3   Finish by stirring through the fresh lemon juice just before serving.

EVERYDAY SPICED OKRA

PREP: 5 MINUTES • COOK: 20 MINUTES • SERVES 4

Okra, or bhindi, is not an exotic vegetable in India. It is everyday, run of the mill, backbone. The fear that many have of okra is the slime they produce. To avoid this, we slice them and then fry them really, really well. This is not a chuck in the pan and stir fry ingredient. You must persevere through the slime phase of frying to the dry, delicious light at the end of the tunnel.

600g/1lb 5oz okra/bhindi

1 small onion, finely chopped

3 tbsp vegetable oil

2 garlic cloves, chopped

1.5cm/⅝ inch piece of fresh root
    ginger, chopped

1 tsp ground turmeric

½ tsp chilli powder

4 tsp ground coriander

2 tsp garam masala

salt

3 tomatoes, chopped

Rotis (see page 130) or Puris (see
    page 134) to serve

1 Wash, dry and split the okra lengthways, cutting through the flesh about halfway so that one edge is still intact.

2 Fry the onion in the oil over a medium heat until golden brown.

3 Add the garlic and ginger and fry for 1 minute, then sprinkle in the turmeric, chilli powder, coriander, garam masala and salt and cook for a further minute.

4 Drop the okra into the pan and cook for 2–3 minutes, then add the tomatoes and fry for 12–15 minutes until soft and the mixture becomes fairly dry.

5 Serve the okra with puri breads or rotis.

CUMIN WALNUT RUNNER BEANS

PREP: 5 MINUTES • COOK: 10 MINUTES • SERVES 4

I invented this dish in my home kitchen when I had a big bag of walnuts I wanted to use up and not enough beans to feed everyone. I threw it together and it has become something of a signature dish of mine. I love the crunch of the walnut with the soft, sweet bean bite. It's a very simple, throw-together dish, but the rich texture of the walnuts lend it a certain kind of luxury.

4 tbsp vegetable oil

1 tbsp cumin seeds

250g/9oz young runner beans, strings removed, topped, tailed and chopped into thirds

1½ tsp ground cumin

¼ tsp ground turmeric

⅛ tsp chilli powder

100g/3½oz/¾ cup walnuts, roughly chopped into large pieces

3 tbsp honey

½ tsp salt

juice of ½ lemon

1 Put the oil in a large frying pan set over a medium-high heat. When hot, add the cumin seeds and fry until they turn dark brown and become fragrant, then turn the heat down to medium and add the runner beans, ground cumin, turmeric and chilli powder. Fry for 6–8 minutes, stirring regularly, until the beans have turned a nutty brown and softened.

2 While the beans are cooking set a small non-stick frying pan over a medium heat and add the walnuts, honey and salt. Fry for 3–5 minutes until the nuts are fully coated and sticky. Take care that the honey doesn't catch and burn, adding a splash of water if necessary.

3 When the nuts are golden and sticky, put them into the pan with the beans and toss well until everything is fully combined. Finish with a squeeze of fresh lemon juice just before serving.

HOME-STYLE AUBERGINE

Many Indians are vegan. Aubergine/eggplant is India's best-loved vegetable and the reason for this, my Maa and I reckon, is because it is the closest many Indians get to that meat texture. We always fry the aubergine *before* we add our curry spices, unlike in Thai cuisine. This adds a caramelised sweetness to the flesh that does much of the legwork in creating the massive flavours in this dish.

4 tbsp vegetable oil

1 tsp panch phoron

1 large dried red chilli

2 large aubergines/eggplants, cut into long, thin 5cm/2 inch slices

¼ tsp ground turmeric

¼ tsp chilli powder

1 tsp salt

1 tsp caster/granulated sugar

juice of ¼ lemon

250g/9oz canned chopped tomatoes

1 tablespoon chopped coriander/ cilantro leaves

88

1 Put the vegetable oil in a large non-stick frying pan set over a medium-high heat. When hot, add the panch phoron and fry until they start to crackle, then add the red chilli and aubergines and, turning the heat down to low, partially cover and cook for 10 minutes or until the aubergines are golden brown and tender.

2 Stir the ground turmeric, chilli powder, salt, sugar, lemon juice and the canned tomatoes into the aubergine mix and fry for a further 6 minutes until the oil has started to split out of the tomatoes. Garnish with the chopped coriander and serve.

COURGETTE AND BAY

Courgette/zucchini is one of the most lacklustre vegetables if treated with impropriety. It needs to be dealt with delicately, but we believe in the Hindu kitchen that it needs a kick into flavour. Bay is the spice we use to emulate the strong flavours of the meat spice garam masala. This wakes up wonderful aromatics in the squash. A great pairing.

4 tbsp vegetable oil

2½ tsp panch phoron

2 small dried red chillies

1 large white onion, cut in half and
     thinly sliced

1 medium potato, peeled and chopped
     into 2cm/¾ inch chunks

¼ tsp ground turmeric

⅛ tsp chilli powder

200g/7oz canned chopped tomatoes

4 bay leaves

2 large courgettes/zucchini, about
     400g/14oz, chopped into 2cm/
     ¾ inch cubes

1 tsp salt

1 tsp caster/granulated sugar

juice of ½ lemon

90

1 Put the vegetable oil in a large non-stick frying pan set over a medium-high heat. When hot, add the panch phoron and fry until the nigella seeds start to crackle and pop. Turn the heat down to low, add the white onion and dried red chillies and fry for 6–8 minutes or until the onion turns golden brown.

2 Add the cubed potato, ground turmeric and chilli powder and fry gently, partially covered, for 20–25 minutes or until the potatoes are soft and cooked through.

3 Add the tomatoes and fry until the oil starts to split out of them, then add the bay leaves and cubes of courgette. Give everything a good stir together and continue to cook for 10 more minutes or until the courgette is tender. Finish with the salt and sugar and finally stir through the fresh lemon juice just before serving.

PANEER CHEESE

PREP: 25 MINUTES + 1 HOUR PRESSING AND CHILLING
• COOK: 5 MINUTES • SERVES 4

I love to play with paneer. It's the simplest form of cheese making and it's something parents and children can do together – it has all the bonding of baking and the great charm of playing with plasticine. I often add chopped fresh herbs into the paneer to conjure up different flavours. It has that squeaky, halloumi bite when it has been properly made, but sometimes I eat it with lemon juice and herbs as a soft cheese when it has not been fully compressed. Give it a go – invent your own home cheese.

2.25 litres/79fl oz/9½ cups
  full-cream/whole milk

60ml/2fl oz/¼ cup lemon juice
½ tsp salt

1 Pour the milk into a large saucepan set over a medium-high heat and bring up to a slight simmer (just under 95°C/200°F using a food thermometer). Stir occasionally to ensure the milk doesn't catch and scald.

2 Once the milk is up to temperature and looks frothy, remove from the heat and stir in the lemon juice, then cover and set aside for 10–15 minutes.

3 Line a colander with muslin cloth/cheesecloth and set over a large bowl, then carefully scoop out the cheese curds and place them in the colander, letting the whey collect in the bowl underneath.

4 Pick up the muslin cloth and give it a gentle squeeze, helping to remove the excess whey, then open up the cloth and sprinkle the salt over the curds and stir well.

5 With the curds still in the cloth, transfer to a large plate or chopping board. Shape into a rough square and fold the cloth tightly around the curds. Place another plate or chopping board on top and weigh down with a couple of cans. Press for 1 hour, then chill in the refrigerator.

6 Slice into the required size chunks when needed.

MOWGLI PANEER

PREP: 10 MINUTES • COOK: 35 MINUTES • SERVES 4

My mother used to make paneer by splitting milk with lemon juice and hanging the separated mass from the kitchen tap in a big muslin sack. That udder of pendulant promise meant that night was paneer curry night. I wanted to share the joy with my Mowgli clients and this sweet, chunky curry is one of the best gifts I can give.

4 tbsp vegetable oil

1 tsp cumin seeds

1 green chilli, pierced

2 white onions, finely diced

5 garlic cloves, minced

5cm/2 inch piece of fresh root ginger, peeled and grated

½ tsp ground turmeric

¼ tsp chilli powder

1 tbsp garam masala

1 tsp ground coriander

¼ tsp ground fenugreek

3 tsp tomato purée/paste

200g/7oz canned chopped tomatoes

1 tsp salt

1 tsp sugar

100g/3½oz/⅔ cup frozen peas

200g/7oz spinach, washed and drained

250g/9oz Paneer (see page 92)

½ bunch of fresh coriander/cilantro

2 green chillies, deseeded and thinly sliced

1 Put the vegetable oil in a large non-stick frying pan set over a medium-high heat. When hot, add the cumin seeds and fry until they turn dark brown and release their aroma. Add the green chilli and diced white onions and fry for 3 minutes, then add the garlic and ginger and fry until the onions are translucent.

2 Add the ground turmeric, chilli powder, garam masala, ground coriander, ground fenugreek and tomato purée and stir until everything is fully combined.

3 Add the chopped tomatoes, 200ml/7fl oz/scant 1 cup water, salt and sugar, bring up the the boil, then reduce the heat to low and continue to cook gently for 15–20 minutes, stirring occasionally, until you have a thick and creamy sauce.

4 Add the frozen peas and spinach and cook for 2 minutes until the spinach has wilted, then add the paneer and stir well. Continue to cook for 3–5 minutes until the paneer is soft and giving, but no longer as it will become dense and tough.

5 Finish with the fresh coriander and green chilli just before serving.

PANEER SKEWERS

PREP: 10 MINUTES + 30 MINUTES CHILLING •
COOK: 10 MINUTES • SERVES 4

These marinated hunks of paneer are a very common protein-on-stick hit. Here I use peppers to add sweet, moist buffers between the cheese and I have used powerful spices and the acids of the garlic and ginger to penetrate the reluctant paneer. Sometimes a splash of apple juice helps soften in a most delightful way. This paneer is delicious wrapped in a roti (see page 130), with a little slaw (see page 140) on the side.

8 wooden skewers
600g/1lb 5oz Paneer, cut into chunks
    (see page 92)
1 red onion, cut into large chunks
2 different coloured peppers, deseeded
    and cut into chunks
120ml/4fl oz/½ cup mild olive oil
1 garlic clove, crushed

1 tsp grated fresh root ginger
1 tsp salt
1 tsp garam masala
½ tsp chilli powder
2 tsp ground coriander
1 tbsp lemon juice
handful of fresh coriander/cilantro
    leaves, chopped

1 Soak the skewers in water for 30 minutes to prevent them burning.

2 Combine all of the ingredients together in a large bowl, mix well, and cover with cling film/plastic wrap, then refrigerate for 30 minutes.

3 Preheat the griddle/grill pan or barbecue to a high heat.

4 Tightly thread the paneer, onion and peppers on to the skewers and grill over a high heat for around 8–10 minutes, turning every few minutes, until golden.

CREAMY FENUGREEK-SPICED PUMPKIN

PREP: 10 MINUTES • COOK: 35 MINUTES • SERVES 4

Indians love pumpkins. They grow everywhere and we love the way that their sweet, dense flesh holds up to a simmer in this intriguing, delicately spiced milk sauce.

4 tbsp vegetable oil
1 tsp fenugreek seeds
1 large dried red chilli
1 large white onion, chopped into 1cm/½ inch cubes
1 pumpkin, around 500g/1lb 2oz, peeled and chopped into 5cm/ 2 inch chunks

¼ tsp ground turmeric
⅛ tsp chilli powder
1 tsp salt
1 tsp caster/granulated sugar
200ml/7fl oz/scant 1 cup full-cream/ whole milk

1 Put the oil in a large non-stick frying pan and set over a medium-high heat. When hot, add the fenugreek seeds and fry until they turn golden. Add the dried red chilli and the onion and fry for 8 minutes until the onion has softened and turned deep brown.

2 Add the cubed pumpkin, ground turmeric, chilli powder, salt and sugar, partially cover and simmer gently for 20 minutes or until the pumpkin is tender and cooked through.

3 When the pumpkin is soft, turn the heat up to high and pour in the milk. Cook vigorously for a further 5 minutes until the sauce is thick and creamy, then serve.

THE HINDU KITCHEN

4
THE HOUSE KITCHEN

I call myself a curry evangelist because I set out, through my books, my YouTube videos, my building of Mowgli, to show the British public how achievable and simple Indian food really is. It breaks my heart that curry is the UK's number one dish, but only 10 per cent of the population know how to cook it. It is time that curry belonged to my fellow Brits in the way that spaghetti Bolognese is now an established family member, free from fear and confusion.

The curry houses of the high street are places of grace and obeisance. They were created to please the Western palate. Their chefs are great and they, in their kindness, looked at the way we eat in Britain and made the Indian dishes fit. You like meat and you like a thick gravy, so that is what we will do for you. But I won't and Mowgli is the antithesis of a normal curry house.

The names of the dishes are where the difference begins. In India, we don't use the names of dishes that you see on curry house menus. We generally have a 'house' meat curry. This is one that has been tailored and tweaked by generations within that particular family. It will contain the spice blend and balance that that family have loved for centuries and the flavours are nuanced and unique to that home –

fragrant but bespoke. This makes the dish potentially extremely frustrating and unsatisfactory to an Indian from a different spice background. If it does not taste like their grandmother's and mother's, then it tastes wrong. This is how viscerally strong Indians feel about their dishes and why it is important for me to head up my list of home-crafted dishes as 'The House Kitchen'.

My background is north Indian. Specifically, we are Bengali and from Calcutta of old. This means we have a very particular way of cooking and we reach for very different spices and finishing flavours from other areas of India. We love to use mustard paste towards the end of a cook to add zing and heat to a dish, and our headnote spice of choice is panch phoron, which is a Bengali five-spice mix.

If you were to dine in the chaotic privacy of my kitchen after the curtains were drawn and the formality was over, this is how the dishes would taste. They would not taste like the gems of a Punjabi, Gujarati or Bangladeshi home. They are mine, born in the ancient streets of Lucknow and Varanasi and honed in Skelmersdale and Birkenhead by my tyrannical tastebuds and my equally tyrannical matriarchs.

101

HOUSE LAMB CURRY

PREP: 10 MINUTES • COOK: 1½ HOURS • SERVES 4–6

Every Indian home needs an all-guns-blazing rich meat curry. Ordinarily we would only ever cook lamb on the bone, and hence in Mowgli we add marrow bones in for the long simmer. A luxurious richness is brought with the aromatic spicings and I added a sweet headiness by including ground anise and prunes, which turn to a thick, sweet mass in the pan. I love using rotis to mop up the deep, sweet juices.

6 tbsp vegetable oil

1 large white onion, cut in half and thinly sliced

7.5cm/3 inch piece of fresh root ginger, peeled and grated

4 garlic cloves, minced

800g/1lb 12oz diced lamb leg

¼ tsp ground turmeric

¼ tsp chilli powder

200g/7oz canned chopped tomatoes

1 tsp star anise powder

1 tbsp ground cumin

1 tbsp ground coriander

1 tsp ground cinnamon

3 green cardamom pods

4 cloves

125g/4oz prunes

200g/7oz canned chickpeas/ garbanzo beans, drained and rinsed

2 tsp salt

2 tsp sugar

1 small bunch of fresh coriander/ cilantro, leaves and stalks chopped

1 green chilli, deseeded and thinly sliced

Rotis, to serve (see page 130)

1 Put the oil in a large heavy pan and set over a medium-high heat. When hot, add the sliced onion, ginger and garlic and fry for 8 minutes or until the onion has softened and turned golden brown.

2 With the heat still on medium-high, add the diced lamb, ground turmeric and chilli powder and fry for 6 minutes, until the lamb is browned all over.

3 Next add the chopped tomatoes, 500ml/17fl oz/2 cups water, star anise powder, ground cumin, coriander, cinnamon, cardamom and cloves. Bring up to the boil, then reduce the heat to low and simmer gently, partially covered, for 30 minutes.

4 Add the prunes, chickpeas, salt and sugar and continue to simmer for a further 35–40 minutes or until the lamb is cooked through and tender. Finish by stirring through the fresh coriander and green chilli just before serving with fresh rotis.

LAMB KEEMA

In India, we don't really have lamb. Woolly sheep don't make sense in the heat of the East and instead we have a kind of goat-sheep hybrid that is tough and hardy. This is why keema, which translates simply as 'mince', is so common. Mincing tough, gamey meat is the best and quickest way to tenderise it, whereas chunks require hours of simmering when not everyone has hours' worth of fuel.

80ml/2½fl oz/⅓ cup vegetable oil

2 white onions, finely diced

5cm/2 inch piece of fresh root ginger, peeled and grated

3 garlic cloves, minced

500g/1lb 2oz lean lamb mince

200g/7oz canned chopped tomatoes

200g/7oz canned chickpeas/ garbanzo beans, drained and rinsed

¼ tsp ground turmeric

¼ tsp chilli powder

2 tsp ground cumin

2¼ tsp garam masala

1 tsp salt

2 tsp sugar

50g/2oz/⅓ cup frozen peas

1 large green chilli, deseeded and finely sliced

½ small bunch of fresh coriander/ cilantro, roughly chopped

1 Put the oil in a large heavy pan and set over a medium-high heat. When hot, add the diced onions, ginger and garlic and fry for 6 minutes until the onions are translucent and soft.

2 Add the minced lamb and fry for a further 5 minutes or until the lamb is coloured all over, breaking up any large lumps with a fork. Add the canned tomatoes, chickpeas, ground turmeric, chilli powder, ground cumin, garam masala, salt, sugar and 200ml/7fl oz/scant 1 cup water and bring up to the boil. Reduce the heat to low, cover and cook gently for 50–60 minutes, stirring occasionally and adding more water if necessary.

3 Five minutes before the cooking time is finished, add the frozen peas and sliced green chilli. Once the peas are cooked, check for seasoning and add more salt if necessary. Finish by stirring through the fresh chopped coriander just before serving.

STAFF MUTTON CURRY

PREP: 20 MINUTES + 2 HOURS MARINATING •
COOK: 2 HOURS 15 MINUTES • SERVES 4

This dish is the ultimate in humble ingredients, but so full of flavour, simplicity and mutton that it positively dazzles after a long, slow simmer. It is perfect to pop in a low oven during a busy evening service. Tables of eager kitchen and waiting staff are seen demolishing pots of this in the tired, wee hours of street eateries across India.

800g (1lb 12oz) boneless leg of
　　mutton, cut into 2.5cm/1 inch cubes
2 tbsp vegetable oil
6 potatoes, peeled and halved
3–4 tsp garam masala
handful of chopped coriander/cilantro
　　leaves, to garnish
Puris, to serve (see page 134)

FOR THE MARINADE
3 tsp ground turmeric
2 tsp chilli powder

2 tsp ground cumin
2 tbsp ground coriander
2 bay leaves
2 green chillies, chopped
3 onions, chopped
6–8 garlic cloves, peeled and chopped
1cm/½ inch piece of fresh root ginger,
　　peeled and chopped
8 whole tomatoes
3 tbsp mustard/canola oil
1 tsp sugar
salt, to taste

1　Wash the mutton pieces and mix with all the marinade ingredients in a large bowl. Add a little salt to taste. Leave for at least 2 hours to marinate (or, if keeping in the refrigerator, for up to 24 hours).

2　Preheat the oven to 190°C/375°F/gas 5. In a heavy casserole dish, heat the vegetable oil to smoking. Cool a little, then add the meat and all the marinade ingredients. Stir-fry for 12–15 minutes.

3　Add the potatoes, garam masala and 450ml/15fl oz/1¾ cups hot water. Stir to mix well, then season to taste. Cover and cook in the oven for 2 hours. Remove from the oven every so often to check the liquid level – the gravy should be just coating the meat – add a touch of water if you're worried, then return to the oven.

4　Remove the curry from the oven and garnish with chopped coriander leaves. Serve with puri breads.

ROADSIDE LAMB SHANKS

PREP: 30 MINUTES + 1 HOUR MARINATING •
COOK: 2 HOURS 40 MINUTES • SERVES 8

This is a perfect busload-banqueting sharing dish. I love lamb shanks. They are bulky little blighters because they carry their bone in and so I choose cauldron-size cooking pots for this dish. The bones release so much flavour and the hard-working flesh falls apart into tender, succulent submission after the 2-hour cook.

3 lamb shanks, 2kg/4lb 8oz in all
Mowgli Slaw (see page 140) or salad,
    to serve

1 tsp chilli powder
2 tbsp vegetable oil
salt

FOR THE MARINADE
1 tbsp white poppy seeds
4 x 2.5cm/1 inch cinnamon sticks
2 black cardamom pods
6 green cardamom pods
4 cloves
2 tbsp fennel seeds
1 tbsp cumin seeds
1 tsp Szechuan pepper
2 onions, chopped
8 garlic cloves, chopped
2.5cm/1 inch piece of fresh root
    ginger, peeled and roughly chopped
3–4 green chillies, chopped
6–8 fresh mint leaves
2 tsp ground turmeric

FOR THE SAUCE
2.5cm/1 inch piece of fresh root
    ginger, peeled and roughly chopped
6 garlic cloves, chopped
2 tbsp vegetable oil
2 bay leaves
3 onions, finely chopped
350g/12oz/1⅓ cups plain yogurt
1 tsp ground turmeric
2 tsp gram/chickpea flour
2 tsp chilli powder
2 tbsp ground coriander
1 tsp ground cumin
few saffron strands
few drops of rosewater

1 With a small knife or skewer, make deep holes evenly all over the shanks.

2 To start the marinade, in a frying pan over a low heat, toast the poppy seeds, cinnamon sticks, cardamom, cloves, fennel, cumin and pepper. Grind the toasted spices to a fine powder in a pestle and mortar or spice grinder.

3   Add the onions, garlic, ginger, chillies and mint to a food processor and blend to a fine paste. Mix with the turmeric, chilli powder, vegetable oil and salt to taste, then add the ground toasted spices and mix again. Rub the marinade well into the meat and leave for about an hour or longer (or, if keeping in the refrigerator, for up to 24 hours).

4   Preheat the oven to 190°C/375°F/gas 5.

5   Put the lamb on a baking sheet and cook in the oven for about 20 minutes.

6   Meanwhile, make the sauce. Using a pestle and mortar, blend the ginger and garlic together to a paste. Heat the vegetable oil in a deep ovenproof pan. Add the bay leaves and onion, and cook until the onions turn light brown, then add the ginger and garlic paste. In a separate bowl, mix the yogurt with all the remaining sauce ingredients except for the rosewater. Take the onion pan off the heat and add the spiced yogurt. Mix well, then return to the heat and simmer gently for 2–3 minutes. Add 350–450ml/12–15fl oz/1½–1¾ cups water and bring back to a simmer.

7   At this point, the lamb should have finished its 20 minutes. Remove it from the oven and place the lamb and its cooking juices into the deep pot with the sauce. Remove any excess fat. Add salt to taste and then finally the rosewater, cover the pot and return to the oven. Reduce the temperature to 180°C/350°F/gas 4 or lower, and cook for about 2 hours, occasionally ladling the sauce over the lamb.

8   Remove the lid, baste, and return to the oven for another 15–20 minutes, or until the meat is very soft and tender.

9   Serve with a fresh crunchy Mowgli Slaw (see page 140) or your choice of salad.

AGRA GINGER CHICKEN

PREP: 10 MINUTES • COOK: 1 HOUR • SERVES 4–6

This is a very cleansing, light chicken curry that finds its roots in Agra – an area interesting in that it is slightly touristy, so the curries there can be unusually delicate and kind. Ginger in its fresh form is something that instantly makes a chicken curry accessible and fresh. Agra street food stalls with their banana leaf bowls full of this bright red chicken curry leave me with fonder memories than the Taj Mahal itself.

80ml/2½fl oz/⅓ cup vegetable oil
2 large white onions, cut in half and
   thinly sliced
5cm/2 inch piece of fresh root ginger,
   peeled and grated
6 garlic cloves, minced
3 tbsp garam masala
4 green cardamom pods
2 cinnamon sticks
½ tsp ground turmeric
¼ tsp chilli powder

750g/1lb 10oz bone-in chicken thighs,
   quartered
400g/14oz canned chopped tomatoes
1 tsp salt
1 tsp sugar
200g/7oz baby spinach, washed
zest of 1 lime
1 small bunch of fresh coriander/
   cilantro, leaves and stalks
   roughly chopped

1 Put the oil in a large heavy pan and set over a medium-high heat. When hot, add the sliced onions, ginger and garlic and fry for 8 minutes until the onions have softened and turned a deep golden brown.

2 Add the garam masala, cardamom, cinnamon, turmeric, chilli powder and the chicken thighs and fry for 5 minutes or until the chicken starts to brown, stirring so it is well coated with the spices.

3 Add the canned tomatoes, 450ml/15fl oz/1¾ cups water, salt and sugar and bring up to the boil, then reduce the heat to low and simmer gently for 35–40 minutes or until the chicken is cooked through and tender. Finish by adding the baby spinach and lime zest to the curry and when the spinach has wilted, stir through the chopped coriander. Add more water if necessary to loosen to your taste just before serving.

MOTHER BUTTER CHICKEN

This is a Mowgli favourite. What makes it so addictive is the tang of the tandoori dressing marinade. I only make this at home when we have guests, otherwise the uncompromising aromas waft up the drive and can frighten the neighbours.

5 tbsp vegetable oil

2 large white onions, cut in half and thinly sliced

5cm/2 inch piece of fresh root ginger, peeled and grated

6 garlic cloves, grated

2 tsp ground cumin

2 tsp ground coriander

½ tsp ground cardamom

½ tsp ground cinnamon

¼ tsp ground fenugreek

½ tsp ground turmeric

¼ tsp chilli powder

2 tbsp tomato purée/paste

400g/14oz canned chopped tomatoes

5 tbsp Greek-style yogurt

2 tbsp tandoori masala

500g/1lb 2oz boneless, skinless chicken breasts, chopped into 5cm/2 inch cubes

2 tsp salt

1 tsp sugar

80g/3oz/⅓ cup butter

1 Put the oil in a large heavy pan and set over a medium-high heat. When hot, add the diced onions, ginger and garlic and fry for 8 minutes or until the onions have softened and turned golden brown. Turn the heat down to low and add the cumin, coriander, cardamom, cinnamon, fenugreek, turmeric, chilli powder, tomato purée, canned tomatoes and Greek-style yogurt, stir well and cook for a further 5 minutes. Blend the mixture with a hand-held/immersion blender until it turns into a smooth sauce, then set aside.

2 Rub the tandoori masala into the chicken pieces then, in a separate large non-stick frying pan set over a medium-high heat, fry for 6 minutes or until the chicken starts to change colour and brown at the edges.

3 Add the browned chicken to the blended sauce. Return to a low heat and slowly add up to 500ml/17fl oz/2 cups water to achieve the consistency of sauce that you like. Add the salt and sugar and simmer gently for 15–20 minutes or until the chicken is cooked through. Finish by stirring the butter through to create a thick and creamy sauce. Don't be afraid to add a little more water to loosen the sauce to your taste.

HOUSE CHICKEN CURRY

This chicken curry was the taste of dinner parties when I was growing up in 1970s Skelmersdale. Curry leaf and mustard seed give it a very distinctive South Indian flavour. This spice combination makes it so different to all the other Mowgli dishes.

80ml/2½fl oz/⅓ cup vegetable oil

1½ tsp black mustard seeds

2 large white onions, finely diced

7.5cm/3 inch piece of fresh root
    ginger, peeled and grated

6 garlic cloves, grated

5 fresh curry leaves

4 green cardamom pods

500g/1lb 2oz boneless, skinless
    chicken breasts, chopped into
    5cm/2 inch cubes

2 tbsp ground almonds

100g/3½oz creamed coconut

200ml/7fl oz/scant 1 cup coconut milk

¼ tsp ground turmeric

¼ tsp chilli powder

1½ tbsp garam masala

1½ tbsp ground coriander

2 tsp salt

1 tsp caster/granulated sugar

2 green chillies, deseeded and
    finely sliced

200g/7oz/¾ cup plain yogurt

½ small bunch of fresh coriander/
    cilantro, stalks and leaves
    roughly chopped

1   Put the oil in a large heavy pan and set over a medium-high heat. When hot, add the mustard seeds and fry until they fizz and pop, then add the diced onions, ginger and garlic and fry for 6 minutes until the onions have softened and turned golden brown.

2   Add the curry leaves, cardamom pods and chicken pieces and fry for a further 3–5 minutes until the chicken is fully coated in the spices and browned all over. Turn the heat down to low and add the ground almonds, creamed coconut, coconut milk, 100ml/3½fl oz/scant ½ cup water, turmeric, chilli powder, garam masala, ground coriander, salt and sugar and cook, covered, for 45–50 minutes until the chicken is cooked through and tender.

3   Once the chicken is cooked through, add the green chilli and yogurt and give everything a good mix together. Loosen with a little more water if necessary. Finally stir through the fresh coriander just before serving.

BUNNY CHOW

PREP: 15 MINUTES • COOK: 1¼ HOURS • SERVES 4

This dish was devised by railway workers who used to carry their curry to work in a hollowed-out bread loaf. The heat of the chilli is balanced by a little sweetness from the fruit and the bread casing makes a little chicken go a long way!

3 tbsp vegetable oil

2 small white onions, finely diced

5cm/2 inch piece of fresh root ginger, peeled and grated

3 garlic cloves, minced

1¼ tbsp garam masala

2 tsp ground cinnamon

1½ tbsp ground cumin

1 scotch bonnet chilli, deseeded

400g/14oz skinless and boneless chicken thighs, chopped into 5cm/2 inch cubes

1 skinless chicken breast, chopped into 5cm/2 inch cubes

400g/14oz canned chopped tomatoes

½ tsp ground turmeric

¼ tsp chilli powder

3 star anise

125g/4oz/generous ½ cup dried prunes

2 loaves of white bread, cut in half and hollowed out

1 bunch of fresh coriander/cilantro, leaves and stalks roughly chopped

3 red chillies, deseeded and sliced

1 Heat the vegetable oil for 20 seconds in a large non-stick frying pan set over a medium heat, then add the chopped onions, ginger and garlic and fry for 6–8 minutes or until the onions are golden brown.

2 Next add the garam masala, ground cinnamon, ground cumin and the scotch bonnet, give everything a good mix together and then add the chicken thighs and breast. Continue to cook on a medium heat for about 5 minutes, tossing the pan regularly, until the chicken has browned.

3 Add the chopped tomatoes, ground turmeric, chilli powder and 200ml/7fl oz/ scant 1 cup water and reduce the heat to low. Simmer gently for 30 minutes, then add the star anise and prunes and continue to simmer for a further 30 minutes until thick and rich. Add more water if necessary, making sure you have a good volume of sauce as a lot will be absorbed into the bread.

4 To serve, fill each of the hollowed out bread halves with the bunny chow and garnish with the fresh coriander and sliced red chillies.

Pictured overleaf, left

VEGAN BUNNY CHOW

PREP: 10 MINUTES • COOK: 45 MINUTES • SERVES 4

Our chicken bunny chow is a show stopper, but the truth is that the lunch breaks of the Durban Indian are often an entirely vegan affair. The critical part of this dish is the loose and punchy sauce that is absorbed into the bread. The oozing spiced bread then becomes the focus and the chickpeas/garbanzo beans are along for the ride.

3 tbsp vegetable oil

1 tsp cumin seeds

2 bay leaves

2 white onions, finely diced

5cm/2 inch piece of fresh root ginger, peeled and grated

3 garlic cloves, minced

1½ tbsp garam masala

1 tsp ground cumin

1 tsp ground coriander

⅛ tsp chilli powder

¼ tsp ground turmeric

2 large Maris Piper potatoes, peeled and cut into 2cm/¾ inch chunks

400g/14oz canned chopped tomatoes

2 x 400g/14oz cans chickpeas/ garbanzo beans, drained and rinsed

3 tbsp strong Darjeeling tea

1 tsp salt

1 tsp caster/granulated sugar

1 small mango, peeled and cut into small chunks

200g/7oz spinach, washed and roughly chopped

1 small bunch of fresh coriander/ cilantro, roughly chopped

1 Put the vegetable oil in a large heavy saucepan set over a medium-high heat. When hot, add the cumin seeds and fry until they turn brown and fragrant, then add the bay leaves, onions, ginger and garlic and fry for 8 minutes until the onions are soft and dark brown.

2 Add the garam masala, cumin and coriander and cook for 2 minutes, then add the chilli powder, ground turmeric, chopped potatoes, tomatoes, chickpeas, Darjeeling tea, salt and sugar and simmer gently for 20–25 minutes until thick and tangy. Add the fresh mango and simmer gently for 5–10 minutes until the mango softens a little.

3 Finish by stirring through the shredded spinach leaves and chopped coriander.

Pictured on previous page, right

GOAN FISH CURRY

PREP: 10 MINUTES • COOK: 30 MINUTES • SERVES 4

Goan curries are typically hot and tangy and I love how uncompromising their sauces can be. I start this dish off with a fried Kashmiri dried chilli to give it a smoked heat, then ginger and black treacle/molasses pack the rest of the sweet, zingy punch.

80ml/2½fl oz/⅓ cup vegetable oil

2 tsp mustard seeds

1 tsp nigella seeds

1 dried red chilli

2 white onions, cut in half and thinly
  sliced lengthways

5cm/2 inch piece of fresh root ginger,
  peeled and grated

4 garlic cloves, grated

650g/1lb 7oz skinned cod or haddock
  fillets, cut into large chunks

½ tsp ground turmeric

200g/7oz canned chopped tomatoes

¼ tsp chilli powder

1 tbsp back treacle/molasses

juice of ½ lemon

1 tbsp soft brown sugar

1 small bunch of fresh coriander/
  cilantro, leaves and stalks
  roughly chopped

1 Put 50ml/2fl oz/¼ cup of the vegetable oil in a large pan set over a medium-high heat. When hot, add the mustard and nigella seeds until they fizz and pop, then turn the heat down to medium and add the dried red chilli, onions, ginger and garlic and fry for 8 minutes until the onions are soft and translucent.

2 Rub the chunks of cod lightly with ground turmeric then, in a separate large non-stick frying pan set over a medium-high heat, add the remaining vegetable oil and, when hot, flash-fry the fish for 1–2 minutes, then set aside.

3 Add the chopped tomatoes to the onions and cook gently for 6 minutes or until most of the liquid has evaporated, then add the chilli powder, treacle, lemon juice and sugar and give everything a good mix together.

4 Gently add 500ml/17fl oz/2 cups water to the dish and simmer for a further 3 minutes. Now add the fish to the sauce and simmer for 8–10 minutes or until the fish is tender and cooked through. Finish with the fresh coriander just before serving. Add more water if necessary to loosen to your taste.

KERALAN BLACK TREACLE SALMON

PREP: 10 MINUTES • COOK: 20 MINUTES • SERVES 2

South India deals most magnificently with sea fish, while Bengalis are kings of the river fish. Sea fish are strong and robust and can take the brave and sassy ingredients of tomato, treacle, ginger and garlic. This recipe is great with any fish or indeed any white meat. It is a good basic South Indian sauce to have up your sleeve to make interesting the blandest of flesh.

2 green cardamom pods, crushed

2.5cm/1 inch piece of fresh root ginger

2 garlic cloves

1 small cinnamon stick

4 skinned salmon fillets

½ lemon

3 tbsp vegetable oil

1 small green chilli, pierced

1 tbsp yellow mustard seeds

200g/7oz canned chopped tomatoes

¼ tsp ground turmeric

½ tsp chilli powder

1 tbsp black treacle/molasses

100g/3½oz spinach, washed
   and shredded

juice of ½ lemon

½ tsp salt

2 tbsp pomegranate seeds

½ bunch of fresh coriander/cilantro,
   roughly chopped

1 In a large pot set over a high heat, add the cardamom pods, ginger, garlic, cinnamon stick and 1 litre/35fl oz/4¼ cups water and bring up to the boil. Reduce the heat to low and add the salmon, ensuring it is completely covered with the liquid. Cover with a lid and simmer gently for 5 minutes or until the salmon is cooked through and tender. Remove the salmon from the liquid and set aside to cool.

2 Put the vegetable oil in a large non-stick frying pan and set over a medium-high heat. When hot, add the green chilli and yellow mustard seeds and fry until the seeds pop and turn dark brown. Turn the heat down to medium and add the chopped tomatoes, ground turmeric, chilli powder and black treacle and continue to cook for 5 minutes.

3 Add the spinach, lemon juice and salt. Once the spinach has wilted down (about 3 minutes), add the poached salmon and cook for 5 minutes, or until the salmon is cooked through.

4 Finish with the pomegranate seeds and fresh coriander just before serving.

THE CLASSIC MOWGLI PRAWN CURRY

This dish comes from the heart and hands of my Aunty Geeta, who is a second mother to me in many ways. She has such a different way of cooking from Maa. Her dishes are sweeter and less 'spicy' – both are wonderful, but with prawns/shrimp the sweet gentility sings. The unusual flavour of this dish comes from the combination of English mustard and tomato. In India generally we cook prawns/shrimp with the shells and heads on as this adds a natural stock. Try it like this if you want the real Aunty Geeta hit.

4 tbsp vegetable oil

1½ tsp panch phoron

1 large green chilli, deseeded and thinly sliced

400g/14oz can chopped tomatoes

400g/14oz raw king prawns/jumbo shrimp

¼ tsp ground turmeric

⅛ tsp chilli powder

1 tsp muscovado sugar

2 tsp English mustard paste

80g/3oz/½ cup fresh or frozen peas

1 tsp salt

1   Put the oil in a large non-stick frying pan and set over a medium-high heat. When hot, add the panch phoron and green chilli and fry for 30 seconds, then add the chopped tomatoes and fry for 5 minutes until the oil starts to separate from the tomatoes slightly.

2   Add the prawns, ground turmeric, chilli powder, sugar and mustard paste and fry for 3 minutes. Then add the frozen peas, 250ml/9fl oz/1 cup water and salt and stir until everything is mixed.

3   Cover and simmer for 6–8 minutes until the prawns are cooked through.

ROASTED PORTUGUESE HALIBUT

PREP: 20 MINUTES + 30 MINUTES MARINATING
• COOK: 45 MINUTES • SERVES 4

The Portuguese occupation had an enormous influence on Goan cuisine. In their wake, they left a trail of subversive ingredient twists, the addition of alcohol and vinegars among them. The splash of sweet sherry here adds a Mowgli sass that I love.

1 large halibut fillet, about 800g/
   1lb 12oz

juice of 1 lemon

salt

1cm/½ inch piece of fresh root ginger,
   peeled and roughly chopped

6 garlic cloves; 4 roughly chopped,
   2 sliced

1 tsp black peppercorns, crushed

50g/2oz/scant ¼ cup butter

1 red onion, finely chopped

¼ tsp ground turmeric

¼ tsp chilli powder

pinch of sugar

2 tbsp sweet sherry

1 green pepper, deseeded and diced

1 red pepper, deseeded and diced

2–3 tomatoes, chopped

200g/7oz canned chopped tomatoes

2 tbsp vegetable oil

few sprigs of fresh parsley, finely chopped

1 Preheat the oven to 180°C/350°F/gas 4. Wash the halibut fillet and pat dry. Use whole or, depending on the size of your oven and your dish, cut in half. Sprinkle with the lemon juice and salt to taste. Make a paste in the blender with the ginger, chopped garlic and black peppercorns and rub this into the fish. Leave to marinate, covered, for about 30 minutes.

2 Meanwhile, melt the butter in a small saucepan, add the sliced garlic and onion and cook for 2 minutes, until translucent. Add the turmeric, chilli powder, sugar and sherry and fry for a minute. Add the green and red peppers and sauté for a minute. Add the fresh and canned tomatoes and stir. Cook over a medium heat for about 15–20 minutes, stirring occasionally, until thick. Taste for seasoning.

3 While this is cooking, heat the oil in a large ovenproof pan or casserole dish. Brown the fish briefly on both sides, taking care not to break it while turning. Top the fish with the thickened sauce and put the dish into the oven for about 15 minutes, covered. Turn up the heat to 190°C/375°F/ gas 5 and cook the fish for another 3–4 minutes, uncovered. Serve immediately, with crusty white bread.

CAULIFLOWER AND EGG CURRY

PREP: 15 MINUTES • COOK: 30 MINUTES • SERVES 4

Cauli and egg work together brilliantly in this bright, bold curry. Boil your eggs, then fry them to give a gnarled, wrinkled finish. These pockets trap the gorgeous rich sauce and that's the charm of the egg curry.

5 tbsp vegetable oil

2 onions, chopped into 1cm/½ inch cubes

5cm/2 inch piece of fresh root ginger, peeled and grated

5 garlic cloves, grated

1 tsp cumin seeds

2 tbsp garam masala

½ tbsp ground cumin

½ tbsp ground coriander

1 tsp ground turmeric

⅛ tsp chilli powder

400g/14oz canned chopped tomatoes

1 small cauliflower, cut into small florets

1½ tsp salt

2 tsp sugar

8 large eggs

1 Put 3 tablespoons of the vegetable oil in a large heavy saucepan and set over a medium heat. When hot, add the diced onions, ginger, garlic and cumin seeds and fry for 8 minutes or until the onions have softened and turned golden brown.

2 Add the garam masala, ground cumin, ground coriander, ground turmeric and chilli powder and stir until everything is fully mixed, then add the chopped tomatoes, cauliflower, 450ml/15fl oz/1¾ cups water, salt and sugar and bring up to the boil. Reduce the heat to low and simmer gently for 10 minutes. Don't over-stir this as you want to keep the cauliflower florets as whole as possible. Loosen with more water if you feel it is getting too dry.

3 While the sauce is simmering, bring a pan of water large enough to hold the eggs up to the boil. Carefully add the eggs and simmer for 8 minutes. When the eggs are cooked, run under cold water and peel them from their shells.

4 Put the remaining vegetable oil in a large non-stick frying pan and set over a medium-high heat. When hot, add the boiled eggs and fry until they become gnarled, cracked and brown. Add the eggs to the curry sauce and bring back up to the boil, then simmer for a further 6 minutes. You can leave them whole, or halve them and allow some of the yolk to melt into the sauce. Add more water if necessary to loosen to your taste before serving.

5

CARBS, SALADS & PICKLES

Goodness, this is the chapter that should have the simplest recipes within, but it is that holy of holies that contains the most demanding and terrifying barometers of how good an Indian cook one really is. The breads of the Indian kitchen are, I suppose, the equivalent of the sponges and fancies crafted in kitchens of the Victorian era. Those cakes and scones were the items by which a woman's culinary worth was judged. Having said that, I suppose the more monied one was, the less it mattered whether you could really get your Mrs Beeton on. Well, in the Indian kitchen, a woman's ability to roll a perfectly round roti, inflate it effortlessly and get a good puri dough were part of what made her marriageable or not. I hate even writing this. It sounds like I'm endorsing it – I'm not. The bridal cattle market, teeth-checking culture that is founded upon the monstrous dowry system is reprehensible and I hope every aspect of it is eradicated entirely. I recount my memories just so that you understand again how important every aspect of food has been, historically and anthropologically, to Indian culture, warts and all.

Bread is not leavened in the heat of the East. High temperatures mean that proving, although attenuated, just takes too long. The long sit of the dough is a luxury that grey skies afford. A long sit in the blazing sun means an instant fermentation and a galloping rate of rot. No. Flour and water need to be instantly combined in one dish, balled up and rolled out immediately. The hot embers of a fire and a flat iron pan are all that are needed to turn this play dough into soft, handkerchief-like flat breads. Remember that Indians eat with their hands. Well, these breads are used in lieu of spoons to scoop sauces and mop platters. The general rule is that one eats vegetable dishes with rotis and puri as the first course of a meal. Meat dishes are eaten with rice after the delicate vegetable course.

Rice is only one kind of rice for us small-minded Indians. Basmati: white as snow and with an aroma of musk. It has just the right level of absorbency, not impenetrable like other long grains. It is loose enough to act as a binder for our sauces rather than being a sticky grain that closes rank on liquid. Stickier rice is great for chopstick cultures where adherent balls can be picked up. In a finger-licking, hand-eating culture, we gently mash the rice into our curry, but want to feel the individual grain. No pressure folks, but you take your reputation in your hands in this carbs section.

Indian salads are very simple and are not generally lettuce or green-leaf based. Green, succulent leaves with their fragile nature do not thrive or survive long in the heat of India and so it is the more robust, sliceable ingredients that tend to make the salad grade. Onions, tomatoes, lemon or lime and coriander/cilantro get you most of the way there. After that it is the dressing and the powdered spices that give salads their signature twist.

Pickling vegetables in India is a pleasurable and important way of creating culinary adventure in the kitchen. Through the long, hot summers there are few fresh vegetables and so it is critical to preserve them while they are in abundance. We generally preserve them with oils and spices as India was never a place for the abundance of grapes and the vinegars made from them.

ROTIS

PREP: 30 MINUTES + 15 MINUTES RESTING
• COOK: 5 MINUTES • MAKES 6–8 ROTIS

These unleavened flatbreads are made fresh in every Indian home each night. They are made from simple ingredients, but fiendishly difficult to roll. If they are not perfectly circular and an even thickness, they won't inflate, and an uninflated roti is an excruciating failure in the tyranny of the domestic Indian kitchen. A *tawa* is a flat iron pan on which the roti is sealed over a high heat. These pans are heirlooms – the older the better. We in India finish the rotis over an open fire, but flashing the sealed rotis over a gas ring works a treat.

380g/13½oz/2½ cups wholemeal/
   whole-wheat flour

½ tsp salt
1 tbsp vegetable oil

1 In a large mixing bowl add the flour, salt and vegetable oil and combine. Start mixing and add a little water, then keep mixing and continuing to add up to 240ml/8½fl oz/1 cup water until it forms a dough. Knead the dough for 5 minutes until it turns soft and smooth. Leave the dough to rest for 15 minutes under a damp cloth.

2 Start making ping pong-size balls by rolling pieces of dough in the palms of your hands. Flatten the ball, sprinkle some wholemeal flour on the ball and a little on your work surface.

3 Set a tawa over a medium-high heat (if you don't have a tawa, use a medium-size non-stick frying pan) and while it's warming up, start rolling your rotis. As you roll your roti it should be moving in a slight circular motion. Keep rolling until you have a flat circle. If the roti starts to stick, just sprinkle over a little more flour.

4 Place the roti on your pan. You want the first side to be about a quarter cooked and the time of this will vary. Turn the roti over and cook the other side. You want this side a little more cooked than the first, with light brown spots.

5 Now take the roti with a pair of tongs and carefully place over your gas flame burner. The roti will start to puff up. Turn it over with the tongs and set it back on the flame – it will puff more. Be careful not to burn the rotis and make sure you don't overcook it as it will turn hard. Serve the rotis straight away.

BHATURA

Bhatura and chickpea/garbanzo bean curry is known as 'chole bhatura' and is as much an essential marriage in the Indian street food scene as fish and chips or bacon and eggs. These breads are so deeply soft and delicious and are different from the puri (see page 134) in that they are slightly leavened and have the addition of yogurt, which gives flavour and weight.

1 tsp sugar

2 tsp fast-action/instant active
  dried yeast

240g/8½oz/generous 1½ cups
  plain/all-purpose flour, plus extra
  for rolling

1½ tbsp plain yogurt

1 tbsp melted ghee

pinch of salt

vegetable oil, for frying

1   In a large mixing bowl combine 175ml/6fl oz/⅔ cup warm water with the sugar and dried yeast. Mix with a spoon and leave for 5 minutes until the mixture starts to froth and bubble.

2   Add the flour, yogurt, ghee and salt and mix well until it forms a dough. Add a splash more water if necessary until you have a nice soft dough, then knead well for at least 8 minutes. Cover with a damp cloth and leave to prove for 30 minutes or until it has increased in volume slightly.

3   Divide the dough into eight equal-size portions. Lightly flour your work surface and roll each portion into a 14cm/5½ inch circle and set aside.

4   Take a large non-stick frying pan and set over a medium heat. Add about 5cm/ 2 inches of vegetable oil. To check the oil is ready for frying, take a little piece of the dough and drop it into the oil. It should sizzle and float to the top.

5   Fry the bhaturas one at a time, flipping over once, until they are golden brown all over. Drain on paper towels and serve immediately.

PURIS

Puris are the taste of celebration for my family. They are a similar dough base to the roti bread, but you want a tighter dough and the balls that you will roll are about half the size. They are usually fried in ghee and so are not a bread for daily consumption, instead they are often made for large parties, puja festivals and weddings. The reason for this is that they are much quicker to make, frying in seconds, while rotis are healthier, but require time. The conveyor belt of puri-making matriarchs in my family was a thing of frenzied, golden beauty.

310g/11oz/generous 2 cups
  wholemeal/whole-wheat flour,
  plus extra for dusting

½ tsp salt
vegetable oil, for deep frying

134

1 In a large mixing bowl add the flour and salt and make a small well in the middle. Add a little water into the well and start mixing. Continue to mix while gradually adding up to 100ml/3½fl oz/scant ½ cup water until it forms a dough.

2 Put the dough on a floured work surface and knead for 5 minutes until it turns soft and smooth. Cover with cling film/plastic wrap and leave in the refrigerator to rest for 15 minutes.

3 Remove from the refrigerator and split the dough into eight pieces, then roll into balls in the palms of your hands. Flatten the balls, sprinkle with some extra flour and roll into 2mm/⅛ inch thick discs.

4 Set a wok over a medium heat and add 2.5cm/1 inch of vegetable oil. You will know when the oil is hot enough when a breadcrumb dropped into the wok sizzles and turns golden brown.

5 Lower each puri into the oil one at a time, taking care as the oil will be hot. Fry for 40–50 seconds on each side – they will puff up and turn golden brown when done. Remove from the hot oil with a slotted metal spoon and set aside on a paper towel. Eat immediately.

SEV NOODLES

These crunchy, fine, little noodles are the backbone of any chat dish and are fiendishly difficult to make. You will need a sev noodle maker if you want to attempt it. Most Indians buy them. They are made from gram flour – ground chickpeas/garbanzo beans – so are gluten free and wonderfully nutty in flavour. You can omit the chilli powder if you want a mild sev that has much less to say for itself. The very fine noodles are called 'nylon' sev; a charming endorsement of all things '40s.

vegetable oil
120g/4oz/1 cup gram/chickpea flour
¼ tsp ground turmeric

1 tsp chilli powder
¼ tsp salt

1   Take a medium-size mixing bowl and lightly grease the bottom with a little oil, then add the gram flour, ground turmeric, chilli powder and salt and mix until everything is fully combined.

135

2   Add 1 tablespoon of vegetable oil and mix until it forms a soft dough. Now add water 1 tablespoon at a time until it makes a dense, tight dough, then knead for 3–5 minutes until the dough firms up. If the dough sticks to your hands, lightly grease the palms of your hands with a little oil. Once kneaded, divide the dough into two equal portions and set aside.

3   Lightly oil the inside of your sev noodle maker and insert one of the balls of dough. Take a large non-stick frying pan and set over a medium heat. Add about 2.5cm/1 inch of vegetable oil. To check if the oil is ready for frying, take a little piece of dough and drop into the oil – it should sizzle and float to the top, but not change colour.

4   When the oil is ready, hold the noodle maker over the frying pan. Turn the handle and when the noodles start coming out into the pan, slowly move the sev maker in a circular motion. When you have completed one full circle, stop.

5   Fry the noodles for 30 seconds on each side or until they are golden brown. Using a slotted spoon carefully remove the noodles and leave to drain on paper towels. Leave to cool completely.

MOWGLI BLACK CARDAMOM RICE

PREP: 5 MINUTES + 15 MINUTES STANDING
• COOK: 15 MINUTES • SERVES 4

This is the rice that my family have made for over a hundred years. This combination of black cardamom and fried cumin seeds produce a multi-layered aroma to the basmati rice, which makes it so delicious that it is a dish in itself. You need to use basmati – it is as white as snow and has a hint of musk that weaves wonderful magic with the black cardamom.

190g/6½oz/scant 1 cup basmati rice
3 black cardamom pods

1 tbsp vegetable oil
1 tsp cumin seeds

1 Rinse the rice under cold running water until the water runs clear, then leave to drain.

2 Put the rice in a saucepan with the cardamom pods and 450ml/15fl oz/ 1¾ cups water.

3 Bring up to the boil, then simmer for about 10 minutes, uncovered, until almost dry with a dimpled surface.

4 Cover the pan tightly, remove from the heat and leave to stand for 15 minutes.

5 Set a small frying pan over a medium heat and add the oil. Once hot, add the cumin seeds and fry until they turn dark brown and release their flavour, then remove from the heat.

6 Stir the fried seeds though the rice and gently fluff up the grains with a fork before serving.

ALOO KEEMA CHOP

PREP: 30 MINUTES + 20 MINUTES CHILLING •
COOK: 25 MINUTES + 5–6 MINUTES PER BATCH • MAKES 12 CHOPS

I love the word 'chop' in the Indian context. In the West, a chop puts me in mind of a conservative slab of red meat. To Indians, it is the equivalent of a massive, oozing, flavour-grenade croquette. They are typically minced meat and mashed potato concoctions, spiced to the gills and hot as you like. They are breadcrumbed and fried, shameless and utterly breathtaking.

½ tsp cumin seeds
5 potatoes, boiled, peeled and mashed
salt
2 green chillies, chopped
2 sprigs of fresh coriander/cilantro,
    finely chopped
2 eggs
about 225g/8oz fresh white
    breadcrumbs
vegetable oil, for deep frying

FOR THE FILLING
1 tbsp vegetable oil
1 onion, finely chopped
400–500g (14oz–1lb 2oz) lean
    minced lamb
1cm/½ inch piece of fresh root ginger,
    peeled and chopped
½ tsp chilli powder
½ tsp ground coriander
½ tsp ground cumin
½ tsp garam masala
juice of ½ lemon

1 Toast the cumin seeds and grind to a fine powder.

2 Put the mashed potatoes in a bowl and add salt to taste, the green chilli, ground cumin and fresh coriander and mix well.

3 For the filling, heat the oil in a large frying pan over a medium heat, add the chopped onion and cook for 3–4 minutes until light brown. Add the minced lamb and all of the other filling ingredients apart from the garam masala and lemon juice. Stirring continuously, cook for about 18–20 minutes, until the lamb is cooked through. Add the garam masala and lemon juice and some salt to taste. Put the mixture in a sieve and allow any excess oil to drip out and the mixture to cool.

4 Divide the mashed potato into 12 equal portions and form each into a ball. Put the ball in the palm of your hand and make a depression in it with your forefinger.

Put 1 tablespoon of minced lamb into this depression, and fold the potato over and around it. Flatten with your hands to form a round patty. Do this with all 12 and chill, covered, for 15–20 minutes.

5 Beat the eggs in a bowl and put the breadcrumbs on a flat plate. Heat the oil for deep frying in a heavy wok-style pan over a medium heat. Dip each patty into the egg, then coat with the breadcrumbs. Deep-fry, in batches, for about 5–6 minutes until golden brown. Drain on absorbent paper towels and serve hot with freshly sliced onions or a kachumber salad (see below).

KACHUMBER

PREP: 10 MINUTES • SERVES 4

Go to a meal at any Indian home and there will be a salad like this on the table. The dinner table is not dressed without this offering of freshness and light relief. You can add any variations, but the iconic ingredients are the onions, tomato and cucumber. I think it is from cucumber that this dish derives its name, but there is no evidence for this. Sounds like too much of a mad coincidence not to be true if you ask me.

1 onion, chopped
2 large tomatoes, chopped
½ cucumber, cut into 1cm/½ inch pieces
2 tbsp sprouting beans of any sort
3 tbsp canned sweetcorn
½ green pepper, deseeded and cubed
½ red or yellow pepper, deseeded and cubed

2.5cm/1 inch piece of fresh root ginger, peeled and finely chopped
1 green chilli, chopped
2 garlic cloves, finely chopped
3 tbsp lime juice
1 tsp salt (or to taste)
2 tsp ground cumin, lightly toasted in a dry pan
½ tsp chilli powder

1 Mix all of the ingredients together. (This can be made a day in advance. If you do this, then don't add the lime juice until just before serving.)

2 Serve as a salad with the main course, or with puris (see page 134) on the side to form a kachumber salad wrap.

MOWGLI SLAW

PREP: 5 MINUTES + 15 MINUTES STANDING • SERVES 4

Instead of rice or carbs with my curry, often I have this sweet, toffee-like, mustard-popping slaw. We use red cabbage and onion in Mowgli as red cabbage has a better crunch and less sweetness. The onion is critical. No Indian slaw would be without it.

1 small red cabbage, quartered, cored and finely shredded
2 small red onions, thinly sliced
1 large red chilli, deseeded and thinly sliced
150g/5oz/scant 1 cup raisins

1 bunch of fresh coriander/cilantro, leaves and stalks roughly chopped
4 tbsp Mowgli Salad Dressing (see page 161)
pinch of salt, to taste

1 Combine the cabbage, onions, chilli, raisins and coriander in a large bowl, dress with the Mowgli salad dressing and give everything a good mix together. Season with salt to taste. Allow to stand for 15 minutes before serving.

140

CARROT SALAD

PREP: 5 MINUTES + 10 MINUTES STANDING • SERVES 4–6

Carrots in an Indian street market are unrecognisable from their Western cousins. They are often deep red and are as sweet as fruit. For this reason, carrots feature more in salads and desserts than in curry. Never the bridesmaid, always the bride.

5 large carrots, peeled and grated
1 small bunch of fresh coriander/cilantro, leaves and stalks roughly chopped, plus extra to garnish

75g/2½oz/½ cup peanuts, coarsely ground in a pestle and mortar
juice of ½ lemon
½ tsp caster/granulated sugar
½ tsp salt

1 In a large bowl mix all of the ingredients well and let stand for 10 minutes to allow the carrots to release their natural flavour. Mix again just before serving and garnish with a little fresh coriander.

CHINESE LETTUCE SALAD

These big, crunchy, moist leaves are not a common Indian ingredient. They are, however, my favourite salad leaf. They are giant, generous, sweet torpedoes that work as well in salads as they do in soups or stir-fries. This salad formula is entirely transferable to your favourite leaves.

142

1 tbsp vegetable oil
½ tsp mustard seeds
2 small Chinese lettuces, halved and
   finely shredded
1 red pepper, deseeded and
   thinly sliced
1 small red chilli, deseeded and
   thinly sliced

½ small bunch of fresh coriander/
   cilantro, leaves and stalks
   roughly chopped
¼ tsp chat masala
1 tbsp lemon juice
pinch of salt

1 Put the vegetable oil in a small frying pan set over a medium-high heat. When hot, add the mustard seeds and fry until they begin to fizz and pop. Remove from the heat and set aside until cool.

2 In a large bowl, add all of the remaining ingredients, mix well, check for seasoning and serve immediately.

INDIAN TOMATO SALAD

PREP: 5 MINUTES • COOK: 5 MINUTES • SERVES 4–6

Indian dining tables will always have an onion and tomato salad. We usually pile a little heap of salt on the side of our plate and dip the tomato or onion into it and eat them as separate mouthfuls. Choose the best tomatoes you can for this salad. In the East, tomatoes are as flavourful and as beloved as ripe plums.

8 large, ripe vine tomatoes, thinly sliced

1 small red onion, halved and thinly sliced

½ tsp chat masala

1 tbsp lemon juice

pinch of salt

¼ lime

1 green chilli, finely chopped

1   Arrange the sliced tomatoes on a large serving dish, then add the sliced red onion. Sprinkle over the chat masala, lemon juice and salt just before serving. Squeeze the lime over the salad, and garnish with the green chilli to serve.

GREEN CHILLI PICKLE

PREP: 5 MINUTES + 10 DAYS PICKLING • COOK: 5 MINUTES •
MAKES 1 MEDIUM KILNER JAR

This is supposed to be a mind-blowingly hot pickle, which feeds into that addiction that most of the East have to sheer blinding heat in their food. If you want a milder pickle, then remove all the seeds and the white pith from the chilli and choose big banana chillies instead of the finger sort.

10 tbsp black mustard seeds
400g/14oz chopped green chilli
6 tbsp rock salt
juice of 6 lemons

2 tbsp ground turmeric
450ml/15fl oz/1¾ cups mustard/
canola oil

1 In a pestle and mortar, grind the mustard seeds until they make a coarse powder.

2 In a sterilised glass jar, add the green chillies, ground mustard seeds and salt.

3 Cover the jar tightly with the lid and give everything a good shake, then leave in a quiet corner of the kitchen for 3 days.

4 After 3 days, add the lemon juice and the ground turmeric to the jar and give it a stir with a non-reactive spoon. Replace the lid tightly and again leave in a quiet, undisturbed corner for 2 days.

5 Heat the oil in a frying pan set over a medium-high heat until it just starts to smoke, then remove from the heat and let cool slightly for 10 minutes. When cooled, pour the mustard oil over the pickle, replace the lid tightly and leave for 5 days to let the pickling process happen.

6 After the 5 days has passed you can then store the pickle in the refrigerator for up to 2 months.

146

MOWGLI CHUTNEY

PREP: 5 MINUTES • COOK: 30 MINUTES • MAKES 1¼ CUPS

This is a great tomato chutney that will keep in the refrigerator in a jar for weeks. It is the brave addition of ginger and garlic that elevates tomatoes to the level of Indian chutney here. Along with the hum of cumin that just gets better and stronger as time goes by.

4 tbsp vegetable oil

1 tbsp cumin seeds

1 tbsp black mustard seeds

5 curry leaves

6 large tomatoes, roughly chopped

1cm/½ inch piece of fresh root ginger, peeled and grated

2 garlic cloves, minced

½ tbsp chilli powder

½ tbsp ground turmeric

2 green chillies, deseeded and thinly sliced

1 tsp salt

1 Put the vegetable oil in a large non-stick frying pan set over a medium-high heat. When hot, add the cumin seeds, mustard seeds and curry leaves and fry for around 30 seconds until the cumin seeds turn dark brown and release their fragrance.

2 Add the tomatoes, ginger, garlic, chilli powder, ground turmeric and green chilli and stir well. Turn the heat down to low and fry for 5 minutes, stirring occasionally, until the tomatoes start to soften.

3 Add the salt, then cover the pan and cook gently for 15 minutes until the tomatoes have cooked down and released their liquid. At this point remove the lid and stir until a smooth sauce forms. Continue to cook for a further 5 minutes so the relish thickens slightly. Store in an airtight jar in the refrigerator for up to a month. Once open, refrigerate and eat within a week.

Pictured overleaf: Green Chilli Pickle, bottom left;
Mowgli Chutney, top right

TAMARIND CHUTNEY

This chutney is simple in its ingredients, but the balance is hard to get right. It takes much practice and will become your signature chat dressing. Some like it sweet, some like it hot. In Mowgli, with me at the helm, I like it sweet with the pungent kick of black salt. This is what brings zing to chat.

250g/9oz tamarind, seeds removed
500g/1lb 2oz/2¼ cups caster/
   granulated sugar
1 tbsp ground cumin
1 tbsp salt

½ tsp black salt
1¼ tsp chilli powder
½ tsp freshly ground black pepper
½ tsp ground ginger

1 Break the tamarind into pieces and pour over 475ml/16fl oz/scant 2 cups boiling water. Leave to soak for 1 hour.

2 Using a fork, mash the tamarind into a pulp, then strain through a sieve. Add the sugar to the remaining pulp and mix well, then add all the other ingredients and stir to fully combine.

3 Store in an airtight container in the refrigerator for up to a month.

Pictured on previous page, top left

CORIANDER AND MINT CHUTNEY

PREP: 5 MINUTES • MAKES 1 CUP

If you take one chutney away from this book, please learn this one. It is the cornerstone of any Indian banquet because it brings all the fresh green heat and sharpness that might be missing from any of the dishes. It is used as a seasoning almost, kind of in the way you might use ketchup with a cooked breakfast as a way to make up for any of the flavour gaps between various elements.

1 small bunch of fresh coriander/
    cilantro, leaves and stalks
    roughly chopped
1 small bunch of fresh mint
1 green chilli, deseeded and
    finely chopped

2cm/¾ inch piece of fresh
    root ginger, peeled
1¼ tsp ground cumin
1 tsp ground coriander
juice of ½ lemon
salt

1 Put all the ingredients except the salt into a blender and pulse until a smooth paste forms. Season with salt to your liking. This chutney will keep in the refrigerator for up to 3 days.

151

MANGO PICKLE

PREP: 15 MINUTES + 12 DAYS PICKLING • COOK: 5 MINUTES
• MAKES 1 LARGE KILNER JAR

This is so different to the pickles you find on the curry house carousel. This has a fresh, multi-layered fragrance. The mango must be the raw green sort, which are the miserable little green blighters you find in damp cardboard boxes in Asian grocery stores. They are how Indians bring sharpness to their dishes – they have rather the same role as lemons in the West.

¾ tsp fenugreek seeds

1kg/2lb 3oz raw green mangoes

55g/2oz split mustard seeds

50g/2oz chilli powder

2 tbsp ground turmeric

½ tbsp asafoetida

135g/4½oz rock salt

800ml/28fl oz/scant 3½ cups mustard/canola oil

1　In a pestle and mortar, grind the fenugreek seeds until they make a coarse powder.

2　Wash the mangoes in cold water, then dry thoroughly with a paper towel, making sure there is no moisture left on the mangoes. Using a sharp knife chop the mangoes into bite-size chunks.

3　Put the chopped mangoes into a large bowl and add the ground fenugreek seeds, split mustard seeds, chilli powder, ground turmeric, asafoetida and rock salt. Mix well with a clean spoon, ensuring the mango is fully coated in the spices. Place the pickle mixture into a sterilised glass jar.

4　In a large pan set over a medium-high heat, add the oil and heat until it just starts to smoke, then remove from the heat and allow to cool completely.

5　Once cooled, pour the oil over the pickle mixture, making sure it comes to at least 5cm/2 inches above the top of the pickle. Fasten the jar tightly with the lid and leave in a quiet corner of the kitchen for 10–12 days, stirring every 2 days with a clean spoon, until the mango becomes tender and giving.

6　Once the pickling process is finished, store in the refrigerator for up to 2 months.

MIXED VEGETABLE PICKLE

PREP: 30 MINUTES + 8 HOURS DRYING + COOLING
• COOK: 20 MINUTES • MAKES 2 LARGE KILNER JARS

This is a brilliant way to play creation in your kitchen. A kind of Indian equivalent of piccalilli, it is about the crunch and the tang of sour. I add jaggery, which is a very specialist raw Indian fruit sugar. You can replace this with muscovado/brown sugar and add more if you fancy a kinder, sweeter pickle.

450g/1lb cauliflower, cut into small florets

450g/1lb turnip, peeled and sliced into 2.5cm/1 inch batons

450g/1lb carrot, peeled and sliced into 2.5cm/1 inch batons

4 tbsp garam masala

2 tbsp fenugreek seeds

2 tbsp fennel seeds

2 tbsp mustard seeds

600ml/20fl oz/2½ cups mustard/canola oil

150g/5oz fresh root ginger, peeled and grated

½ tsp asafoetida

3¼ tbsp chilli powder

1¼ tsp ground turmeric

4 tbsp rock salt

400ml/14fl oz/1⅔ cups white wine vinegar

300g/10½oz jaggery

1 Half fill a stockpot large enough to hold the cauliflower, turnip and carrot with water and bring up to the boil. Add the cauliflower and boil for 1 minute, then add the turnip and carrot and boil for a further minute. Drain the vegetables well, then place on a clean paper towel and leave to dry for at least 8 hours. This step is important as any extra moisture can cause the pickle to spoil.

2 In a pestle and mortar, grind the garam masala and the fenugreek, fennel and mustard seeds until they form a coarse powder.

3 In a large frying pan set over a medium-high heat, add the oil and heat until it just starts to smoke, then remove from the heat and allow to cool slightly for 10 minutes.

4 When cooled slightly, add the grated ginger and fry for a couple of seconds, then add the asafoetida, chilli powder, turmeric, salt and the coarsely ground mixed spices.

5 Add the vegetables to the pan and give them a good mix together, ensuring everything is fully coated in the spices.

6 In a separate saucepan set over a medium-high heat, add the white wine vinegar and when it starts to boil, add the jaggery and cook until it is completely dissolved, then let cool for 15 minutes.

7 Once cooled slightly, add the spiced vegetables and mix well. Transfer the pickle to a large sterilised jar, fasten tightly with a lid and leave in a quiet corner of the kitchen for 3 days. This will keep in the refrigerator for 1 month.

YOGURT CHAT CHUTNEY

PREP: 5 MINUTES • MAKES 1 CUP

Yogurt is a most beloved ingredient in India. We often have a bowl of yogurt on the side of our dinner plates to cool and to reset the palate. This sweetened version is the yogurt we use in chat dishes. It brings sweetness and acts as an emollient for all the other singing, dancing, crunching elements.

½ tbsp cumin seeds
250g/9oz/1 cup plain yogurt
1 tsp caster/granulated sugar

2 tsp chat masala
pinch of salt

1 In a small frying pan set over a medium heat, toast the cumin seeds for 1 minute until they release their aroma.

2 Grind the toasted cumin seeds in a pestle and mortar.

3 In a bowl mix together the yogurt, sugar, chat masala, salt and ground cumin seeds. Store in the refrigerator for up to 1 week.

BEETROOT AND GREEN CHILLI PICKLE

PREP: 10 MINUTES • COOK: 10 MINUTES
• MAKES 1 LARGE KILNER JAR

This is a very common way to treat beetroots/beets in India and these kinds of crisp vegetable pickles are extremely popular. The combination of spicings is second nature to Indian grandmothers. The beets need to retain their crunch, while the spicing is sharp and can be carried well by the sugars in the vegetables.

4 tbsp vegetable oil

1 tsp mustard seeds

½ tsp fenugreek seeds

½ tsp asafoetida

2 large green chillies, deseeded and
   thinly sliced

3 dried red chillies

4 large beetroots/beets, peeled and cut
   into 1cm (½ inch) batons

1 tsp salt

1 tsp sugar

juice of 1 lemon

1 Put the oil in a large non-stick frying pan set over a medium-high heat. When hot add ½ teaspoon of the mustard seeds and the fenugreek seeds and fry until the mustard seeds turn grey and the fenugreek a deep golden brown, then add the asafoetida, green chillies and the dried red chillies.

2 Turn the heat down to low and add the beetroot, salt, sugar and lemon juice and continue to cook for 6 minutes or until the beetroot has just started to soften around the edges.

3 Crush the remaining mustard seeds in a pestle and mortar and add them to the beetroot mix, stirring until everything is fully mixed.

4 Place the beetroot pickle in a sterilised jar. It will keep for a week in the refrigerator and can be used straight away.

MOWGLI STICKY SAUCE

PREP: 10 MINUTES • COOK: 5 MINUTES • MAKES 1 CUP

It is so important for a restaurant to have a homemade signature sticky sauce. Well, especially if it is a restaurant that wants to find a way into the hearts of children... and me. In truth Indians don't have a sticky sauce. The closest we have is the tamarind chutney, but I twisted it and created this finger-licking subversion. You could toss any crisp, fried, battered meat into this and take you and your little ones to nirvana.

1 tsp vegetable oil

½ tsp black mustard seeds

1 tsp cumin seeds

135g/4½oz date molasses

50g/2oz tomato ketchup

10g/½oz black treacle/molasses

3 garlic cloves, minced

5cm/2 inch piece of fresh root ginger, peeled and grated

1 tsp garam masala

1½ tsp ground cumin

1 tbsp dark rum

juice of ½ lemon

2 tbsp white wine vinegar

1 Heat the vegetable oil in a large saucepan over a medium heat. When hot, add the black mustard seeds and cumin seeds and fry for about 30 seconds until the mustard seeds pop and turn grey.

2 Next add the rest of the ingredients and stir well until everything is fully combined. Add a splash of water to loosen the mixture up a little if it's too thick.

3 Store the sauce in the refrigerator for up to a week.

TAMARIND TREACLE SAUCE

PREP: 10 MINUTES • COOK: 25 MINUTES • MAKES 1½ CUPS

This sauce was born from my love for treacle toffee. The sweet, dark, rich potency of treacle has always made me think of it as a savoury condiment rather than a sweet ingredient. The spices in this sauce confirm its grown-up savoury role.

1 tsp vegetable oil
½ tsp black mustard seeds
100g/3½oz date molasses
200ml/7fl oz/scant 1 cup tamarind
   water (see page 30)
75g/2½oz tomato ketchup
2 tbsp black treacle/molasses

5cm/2 inch piece of fresh root ginger,
   peeled and grated
1½ tsp garam masala
2 tsp ground cumin
juice of ½ lemon
2 tbsp white wine vinegar
1½ tsp salt

1   Heat the vegetable oil in a large saucepan over a medium heat. When hot, add the black mustard seeds and fry for about 30 seconds until they pop and turn grey.

2   Next add the rest of the ingredients and stir well until everything is fully combined. Cook over a low heat for 15–20 minutes, stirring regularly, until the sauce has reduced and thickened. Add a splash of water to loosen the mixture up a little if it's too thick.

3   Store in the refrigerator for up to a week.

CUMIN RAITA

PREP: 5 MINUTES • COOK: 5 MINUTES • MAKES 2 CUPS

This is a basic way of twisting your yogurt side dish to give it a kick and a punch. It is so important that you fry the cumin seeds so that they are activated into full flavour. The ground coriander adds a herbal note. This is great with vegetable curries and rotis (see page 130). Its flavours are a little lost with the heavier meat curries.

1 tbsp cumin seeds
450g/1lb/1⅔ cups plain yogurt
½ tsp ground coriander

juice of ½ lime
1 small bunch of fresh coriander/
     cilantro, roughly chopped

1 In a small non-stick frying pan set over a medium heat, toast the cumin seeds until they pop and release their fragrant aroma.

2 Transfer the toasted seeds to a bowl with the rest of the ingredients and mix well. Store in the refrigerator for up to 3 days.

MOWGLI SALAD DRESSING

PREP: 5 MINUTES + COOLING • COOK: 5 MINUTES
• MAKES 1 SMALL JAM JAR

Salad dressings in India are usually a squeeze of lemon, a pinch of salt and perhaps chat masala. This is my home-grown salad dressing. I'm not always a fan of desserts, but I have a sweet savoury tooth. Hence you will see that I add the toffee joy of date molasses to many of my basic dressings. You can leave it out if, like Maa, you hate that sweet edge in your main course.

100ml/3½fl oz/scant ½ cup
   vegetable oil
½ tbsp black mustard seeds
20g/¾oz date molasses

2 tbsp white wine vinegar
pinch of salt
½ tsp caster/granulated sugar

1 Heat half of the vegetable oil in a small non-stick frying pan set over a medium heat. When hot, add the black mustard seeds and fry until they fizz, pop and turn grey. Set aside and allow to cool completely.

2 Once cool, either put all of the ingredients in a bowl and whisk vigorously until everything is fully combined, or shake everything together in a tightly sealed jar. The dressing will keep well in the refrigerator for up to 1 week.

161

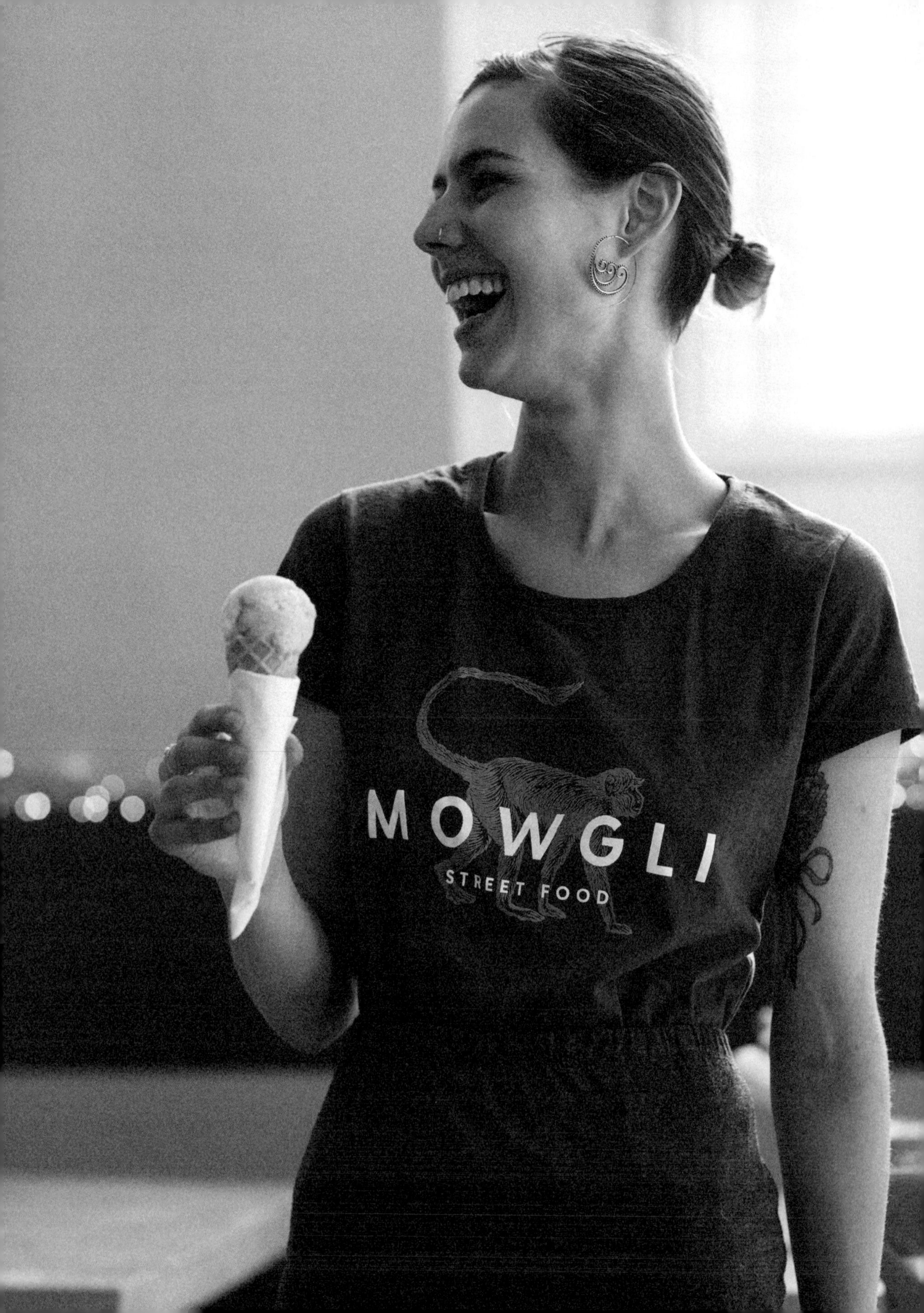
MOWGLI
STREET FOOD

6
DESSERTS

There is a complex dissonance at the heart of Indian dessert culture. Anyone who has walked the length of a British curry mile would think that desserts, sweet meats and all things diabetes-baiting were at the heart of Indian culinary culture. Indian sweet shops are places of immense beauty – gaudy, unashamedly cochinealed beauty. Grimace-inducing greens, bridesmaid pinks and jaundiced yellows are arrayed in the form of Fisher-Price cubes, balls, wheels and squiggles. Okay, so you're beginning to sense a bit of my disdain.

These sweets have a place and that place tends to be in the kitchen halls of weddings and huge ceremonies. Then, teams of master sweet makers will move into a venue with enormous and terrifying vats of hot oil and syrup, and begin to weave their sticky, colourful magic. Some street stalls will similarly specialise in one kind of sweet and, on occasion, a homeward-bound office worker will pick a few gulab jamuns up for a special after-dinner treat. Gulab Jamun is the only concession I make to Indian desserts because they are they most beloved dish of my father, my brother and my husband. Weird how they seem to snag on the Y chromosome in that way. Even stranger that the pet name for them in Bengali is the informal word for 'testicles'.

You see the problem I have is that at the heart of Mowgli is my ambition to bring to the streets a truly home-style Indian kitchen. To demonstrate how Indians really eat in the privacy of their homes, cooking with all that is humble and undressed from their allotments and from the nether regions of their vegetable racks. Gaudy, syrup-laden sweet meats simply do not feature in the day-to-day offerings of the domestic kitchen.

After a meal, we would tend to have yogurt, possibly sweetened yogurt, and fruit. A good home-style rice pudding may feature, but those heaving rainbow platters of sweet stodge are just not how we generally eat. We would want something that gently cleans the palate and leaves us with a note of sweetness, but in terms of belly space, none is really allotted to the dessert course.

The Western appetite has definite belly real estate allotted to the sweet trolley. I ponder and ponder how this enormous difference in taste between India and Britain came about. We had no shortage of sugar in India. Pressed fresh sugar cane juice is one of the most common street stall offerings. It may be that the majority of sweets are milk based, which would turn in the heat. Western desserts are also often baked and Indian cooking culture is stove not oven based. Interestingly, Indians have a terrible propensity for diabetes when they move across to a Western diet and in this it seems as though our very bodies mirror the emphasis of our domestic meal times. We need to listen to our tried-and-tested history more. Take the yogurt route instead of the insulin.

MOWGLI CHOCOLATE CAKE

PREP: 20 MINUTES • COOK: 2 HOURS • SERVES 4

This is a chocolate cake with a warm, spiced twist. I have added cardamom, cloves and nutmeg, but I did toy with cinnamon for a while. Many people struggle with cinnamon and so in a restaurant I thought it would be too divisive. Please play with your own spice balance. This is just an indicator recipe.

200g/7oz dark/bittersweet chocolate, at least 70% cocoa solids
220g/8oz unsalted butter, cubed
¼ tsp ground green cardamom
⅛ tsp ground cloves
¼ tsp ground nutmeg
¼ tsp ground turmeric
¼ tsp garam masala
90g/3¼oz/generous ½ cup self-raising/self-rising flour
90g/3¼oz/generous ½ cup plain/all-purpose flour
¼ tsp bicarbonate of soda/baking soda
220g/8oz/1 cup soft brown sugar
180g/6oz/generous ¾ cup golden caster/granulated sugar

35g/1¼oz cocoa powder
3 eggs
70ml/2½fl oz/¼ cup full-cream/whole milk

FOR THE GANACHE
280ml/9fl oz/generous 1 cup double/heavy cream
220g/8oz dark/bittersweet chocolate, at least 70% cocoa solids

FOR THE GARNISH
2 tbsp chopped pistachios
2 tbsp toasted almonds
1 tbsp dried rose petals
dark/bittersweet chocolate, grated

1 Preheat your oven to 160°C/320°F/gas 3 and butter and line a 20cm/8 inch cake pan, 7.5cm/3 inches deep.

2 Set a heatproof bowl over a saucepan of simmering water. Roughly chop the dark chocolate and add to the bowl, then add the butter, green cardamom, cloves, nutmeg, turmeric, garam masala and 120ml/4fl oz/½ cup water and stir until everything is mixed well and melted, taking care not to overheat. Remove from the heat and set aside.

Continued overleaf

3   In a large mixing bowl, sift together the self raising flour and the plain flour, then add the bicarbonate of soda, soft brown sugar, golden caster sugar and cocoa powder and mix well. In a separate bowl, beat the eggs with the milk.

4   Pour the melted chocolate mixture into the bowl with the dry ingredients and mix well, then add the beaten egg mixture and stir thoroughly until everything is fully mixed and forms a smooth batter. Pour this into your lined cake pan and bake for 1¼–1½ hours until a skewer inserted into the middle of the cake comes out clean. Leave to cool slightly in the tin, then turn out onto a wire/cooling rack and leave to cool.

5   When the cake has completely cooled, carefully cut it in half horizontally using a sharp pastry knife. To make the ganache, set a small saucepan over a medium heat and add the double cream, bring up to the boil, then remove from the heat. Roughly chop the dark chocolate and place it into a mixing bowl. Pour the hot cream over the chocolate and stir well until the chocolate has fully melted.

6   Pour a third of the ganache onto the top of one of the cakes, then place the other cake on top. Pour the rest of the ganache over the cake, letting it run down and around the edges. Use a palette knife/metal spatula to smooth the ganache slightly. Finish by sprinkling the chopped pistachios, toasted almonds, dried rose petals and grated chocolate all over.

GULAB JAMUN

PREP: 30 MINUTES + 3 HOURS STANDING
• COOK: 10 MINUTES • SERVES 10–12

Indians rarely have sweets like this as a dessert. These are festive sweet meats that are complicated to make and hence feature at parties and weddings. The reason I chose to put this on the menu is because there is something about the gulab jamun that just snags on the male DNA. All the lads in my family are addicted, as are my male chefs. Fascinating. I love them, but don't need them like my husband does. It was gulab jamun on the menu, or decree nisi.

FOR THE SUGAR SYRUP
200g/7oz/scant 1 cup caster/
    granulated sugar
few strands of saffron
2 green cardamom pods
¼ tsp rosewater

small pinch of salt
⅛ tsp baking powder
1 tsp ghee, plus extra for greasing
1 tbsp plain yogurt
1 tbsp full-cream/whole milk
vegetable oil, for deep frying

FOR THE DOUGH
125g/4oz/generous 1 cup milk powder
35g/1¼oz/¼ cup plain/all-purpose
    flour

FOR THE GARNISH
1 tsp dried rose petals
2 tsp crushed pistachios

1 Start by making the sugar syrup. Add the caster sugar, 100ml/3½fl oz/scant ½ cup water, the saffron and green cardamom pods to a saucepan set over a medium heat and bring up to the boil. Add the rosewater and continue to cook for a further 2 minutes, then remove from the heat and set aside.

2 Next make the gulab jamun dough. In a mixing bowl add the milk powder, plain flour, salt and baking powder and combine. Add the ghee, yogurt and milk and start to mix with your fingers, bringing the flour together until it forms a soft, sticky dough. Cover and leave to stand for 10 minutes.

3 Once the dough has rested give it a quick mix, then start to shape. Use a little ghee to grease your fingers and roll 12 smooth balls, then set aside.

Continued overleaf

4 Take a medium-size saucepan and set over a medium heat. Add about 5cm/ 2 inches of vegetable oil. To check the oil is ready for frying, take a little piece of the dough and drop it into the oil. It should sizzle and float to the top without colouring.

5 Fry the gulab jamun in three batches until they are cooked and golden brown all over. Drain well on paper towels. Warm the sugar syrup and add the fried gulab jamun, then turn off the heat. Allow to sit for at least 3 hours before serving. Serve the gulab jamun with a little of the syrup, and finish by sprinkling over the rose petals and crushed pistachios.

CARDAMOM COFFEE AFFOGATO

PREP: 5 MINUTES • SERVES 4

I will often ask for one of these when I am in Mowgli and fancy something sweet. Affogato is that wonderful Italian idea of espresso over good vanilla ice cream. Go with the best-quality ice cream you can get. The rose petals pretty it up and pistachio always works so well with cardamom. You don't need them, but they make it very Mowgli.

4 scoops of vanilla ice cream
200ml/7fl oz/scant 1 cup Cardamom Coffee (see page 193)

pinch of dried rose petals
2 tsp chopped pistachios

1 Put a large scoop of ice cream into four dessert glasses or bowls. Pour the cardamom coffee evenly over the four scoops of ice cream. Finish with a pinch of dried rose petals and a sprinkle of the chopped pistachios.

MANGO SORBET

The genius of this light, cleansing sorbet is in the type of mango. The big South American ones give an appley cleanliness, but for a wonderful toffee-like flavour, seek out Alphonso or Kesar. Cans of these mangoes lurk in Asian grocery stores and will forever spoil the shop-bought giants for you.

3 fresh mangoes, peeled, stoned/pitted and cubed or 400g/14oz canned Alphonso or Kesar mango

230g/8oz/scant 2 cups sifted icing/ confectioners' sugar
2 tbsp lime juice

1 Place the cubed mango in a food processor and blend until smooth. Add the icing sugar and fresh lime juice and continue to blend for a further 20 seconds.
2 Transfer the purée to an ice cream maker and churn according to the manufacturer's instructions. Once churned and frozen, store in an airtight container in the freezer for up to 1 month.

WATERMELON SORBET

This is so popular with children and adults alike. It has all the charm of that exotic, heady, pear drop flavour, but it is wonderfully vegan and worthy.

200g/7oz/scant 1 cup caster/ granulated sugar

600g/1lb 5oz diced fresh watermelon
juice of 1 lime

1 Set a saucepan over a medium-high heat and add the sugar and 700ml/24fl oz/ 3 cups water. Bring up to the boil and stir well until the sugar has dissolved. Set aside and allow to cool completely.
2 In a food processor blend the diced watermelon with the sugar syrup and lime juice, then chill in a refrigerator for 2 hours.
3 Once chilled, churn in an ice cream maker according to the manufacturer's instructions. Once churned and frozen, store in an airtight container in the freezer for up to 1 month.

PINK HIMALAYAN SALTED CARAMEL ICE CREAM

PREP: 20 MINUTES + 3 HOURS CHILLING • SERVES 6–8

The pink Himalayan salt contains minerals that give this ice cream a pretty pink glow but this is lost in the cooking, so the ice cream has a gentle latte look. We don't believe in food colouring in Mowgli, so the pink stays in name alone.

250ml/9fl oz/1 cup double/
   heavy cream
200g/7oz/scant 1 cup caster/
   granulated sugar
75g/2½oz/generous ¼ cup unsalted
   butter, cut into cubes

scant ½ tsp pink Himalayan sea salt
500ml/17fl oz/2 cups full-cream/
   whole milk
6 egg yolks
½ tsp vanilla extract

1 Gently heat the cream in a saucepan set over a low heat, then set aside.

2 In a large saucepan set over a medium heat add the caster sugar and cook until the edges begin to melt. Using a metal spoon, gently stir the sugar until it is fully dissolved. Continue to cook for 2–4 minutes. The sugar will get darker and darker as it cooks – you want it to turn a deep dark brown but not be burnt. Once the sugar is golden brown remove from the heat, add the butter and salt and carefully stir until everything is fully mixed and the butter has melted.

3 Put the saucepan back on a low heat, gradually pour in the warm cream and whisk gently to make a caramel. At this point the sugar may harden and form lumps, but will dissolve once the cream heats up. Once smooth, add the milk and stir.

4 In a small bowl whisk the egg yolks for 30 seconds, then slowly pour in a little of the caramel, stirring constantly. Using a spatula, pour the egg and caramel mixture back into the saucepan and cook gently, stirring constantly, until the mixture reads 75°C/165°F on a thermometer.

5 Pour the mixture through a fine sieve into a bowl and chill for at least 3 hours in a refrigerator. When the mixture has cooled, churn in an ice cream maker according to the manufacturer's instructions. Once churned and frozen, store in an airtight container in the freezer for up to 1 month.

Pictured on previous page, bottom right

CARDAMOM CUSTARD TART

PREP: 30 MINUTES • COOK: 1 HOUR • SERVES 6–8

This is such a great variation on the comfort food of our grandmothers' generation. Cardamom works tremendously well in any dishes that are milk based; the aromatic oils in the spice seem to bring custards alive. The other spices you need to play with – omit or enhance as your taste demands – but it is the sprinkle of cardamom at the end that wakes the pudding up in eastern climes.

FOR THE PASTRY

145g/5oz/generous ½ cup cold unsalted butter, cut into small cubes

250g/9oz/1⅔ cups plain/all-purpose flour

¼ tsp ground cloves

⅛ tsp ground ginger

¼ tsp ground cinnamon

¼ tsp ground nutmeg

110g/3¾oz/½ cup caster/granulated sugar

1 egg, beaten

1 tbsp full-cream/whole milk

FOR THE CUSTARD

250ml/9fl oz/1 cup double/heavy cream

250ml/9fl oz/1 cup full-cream/whole milk

1 vanilla pod/bean, split

8 large egg yolks

100g/3½oz/scant ½ cup caster/granulated sugar

2 green cardamom pods, crushed

2.5cm/1 inch piece of fresh root ginger, peeled

1 whole nutmeg

1 clove

2 black peppercorns

1 small bay leaf

3 sprigs of fresh thyme

¼ tsp rosewater

⅛ tsp ground turmeric

1 tbsp ground cardamom, plus extra to sprinkle

1 Start by making the pastry. Rub the cold butter into the flour and ground spices with your fingertips until it starts to resemble breadcrumbs. Add the sugar, egg and milk and gently bring together until it forms a smooth dough.

2 Lightly flour your work surface and roll the pastry out to a thickness of 3–4mm/⅛–¼ inch, then line a 20cm/8 inch tart pan, leaving about 3cm/1¼ inches of pastry overhanging the edge of the pan. Refrigerate for 30 minutes.

Continued overleaf

3 Preheat your oven to 180°C/350°F/gas 4. Take your pastry case out of the refrigerator, prick all over with a fork and line with baking parchment, then fill with baking beads. Blind bake for 20 minutes, then remove the baking beads and parchment and bake for a further 15 minutes or until it is golden brown. Remove from the oven and lower the temperature to 140°C/275°F/gas 1.

4 To make the custard, put the cream, milk and vanilla pod in a medium saucepan set over a medium heat and bring up to the boil. In a mixing bowl, beat the egg yolks with the sugar until pale white, then pour a little of the hot cream mixture over the egg yolks and mix well. Pour this back into the saucepan, then add the rest of the custard ingredients. Reduce the heat to low and cook, stirring continuously, for a further 5 minutes. Strain the custard into a pouring jug and skim off any froth or bubbles.

5 Carefully pour the custard into the case, then place the tart case on a shelf in the middle of your oven. Bake for 40–45 minutes or until just set – there should still be a slight wobble to the custard as it's removed from the oven.

6 Trim off the overhanging edges, then leave to cool completely. Finish with a sprinkle of ground cardamom just before serving.

MOWGLI ROCKY ROAD

PREP: 10 MINUTES + 2 HOURS SETTING
• COOK: 5 MINUTES • SERVES 6–8

This is something I developed solely because my daughters wanted to see it on the menu. It has an almost mulled, spice edge that makes it quite grown up, complex and sophisticated. This made it a source of disappointment for my girls. They wanted the marshmallows and syrup and to be able to down five in a row without engaging palate or brain.

150g/5oz/generous ½ cup softened
   unsalted butter
350g/7oz dark/bittersweet chocolate,
   at least 70% cocoa solids, broken
   into pieces
3 tbsp golden/light corn syrup
½ tsp ground cardamom
½ tsp ground cinnamon
100g/3½oz digestive biscuits/
   graham crackers

100g/3½oz ginger snaps
50g/2oz dried cherries
50g/2oz dried cranberries
75g/2½oz mini marshmallows
30g/1oz coconut flakes
30g/1oz crystallised ginger,
   cut into pieces
2 tsp dried rose petals
2 tsp chopped pistachios

1 Grease and line a square 25cm/10 inch baking pan. Place a heatproof bowl over a pan of simmering water, making sure the water doesn't touch the bottom of the bowl. Put the butter, dark chocolate, golden syrup, ground cardamom and ground cinnamon in the bowl and stir well until the butter and chocolate have melted.

2 Put the digestive biscuits and ginger snaps into a freezer bag and bash with a rolling pin – you want large, chunky pieces of biscuit. Once the chocolate mixture is fully melted, remove from the heat and add the crushed biscuits, cherries, cranberries, marshmallows, coconut flakes and crystallised ginger and mix well.

3 Pour into the lined cake pan, then sprinkle over the dried rose petals and chopped pistachios. Set in the refrigerator for at least 2 hours before turning out and cutting into slices.

CHOCOLATE CHAT BOMBS

PREP: 30 MINUTES + COOLING • COOK: 5 MINUTES • SERVES 2

I developed these for my and my friends' children. We experimented with these a lot in Mowgli, but I have yet to put them on the menu because chocolate is not an Indian ingredient. In the heat of the East, it melts, becoming crystalline and white. I take these decisions about the menu hideously seriously. My kids hate me for it!

150g/5oz dark/bittersweet chocolate, broken into pieces
10 pani puri (see pages 30–31)
flesh and seeds from 4 passion fruit
2 tbsp chopped pistachios

FOR THE GANACHE
110ml/3¾fl oz/scant ½ cup double/ heavy cream

110g/3¾oz dark/bittersweet chocolate
½ tsp dried rose petals, plus more to garnish

FOR THE WHIPPED CREAM
120ml/4fl oz/½ cup whipping cream
2 tsp icing/confectioners' sugar, sifted
⅛ tsp ground cinnamon
1 vanilla pod/bean, seeds only

1 Set a small heatproof bowl over a saucepan of simmering water. Put the chocolate in the bowl and stir until fully melted.

2 Carefully take each pani puri and coat in the melted chocolate, then set aside on baking parchment and allow to cool fully.

3 While the pani puri are cooling, start to make your chocolate ganache by setting a small saucepan over a medium heat. Add the double cream, bring up to the boil, then remove from the heat. Roughly chop the dark chocolate and place into a mixing bowl. Pour the hot cream over the chocolate, add the dried rose petals and stir well until the chocolate has fully melted. Set aside and allow to cool. Meanwhile, whip your cream with the other ingredients in a large mixing bowl until it forms stiff peaks.

4 To assemble, carefully break a hole in the top of each pani puri. Start by adding the fresh passion fruit and chopped pistachios until they fill the pani puri by a third, then spoon in the chocolate ganache until each pani puri is two-thirds full. Finish by filling them the rest of the way up with the whipped cream. Garnish with dried rose petals and chopped pistachios.

CARROT HALWA

Carrots in India are more like fruit than an anodyne root vegetable. They are red and full of sweet, deep flavour, which makes them excellent ingredients in desserts. This great recipe showcases carrots in a very different way. It's a kind of flour-free, sticky carrot cake. And it's heavy – you only need a small slice... or two.

2 tbsp vegetable oil

2 cardamom pods

500g/1lb 2oz carrots, peeled, washed and coarsely grated

700ml/24fl oz/3 cups full-cream/ whole milk

250g/9oz/generous 1 cup caster/ granulated sugar

50g/2oz/¼ cup raisins

pinch of saffron threads

1 Put the vegetable oil in a large high-sided frying pan set over a medium-high heat. When hot, add the cardamom pods and fry until they become fragrant – about 30 seconds. Add the grated carrot to the pan and fry for 4 minutes.

2 Add the milk and bring up to the boil. While boiling, stir constantly for 5 minutes, ensuring the milk doesn't catch on the bottom of the pan. Turn the heat down to low and simmer for 1 hour, uncovered, making sure to stir regularly.

3 After an hour the milk should have reduced by about a half. At this point add the caster sugar, raisins and saffron threads, then turn the heat up to medium and continue to cook for a further 15 minutes, stirring regularly, until the halwa is glossy and thick.

4 You can serve the halwa warm or cold, and it will keep in the refrigerator for up to 3 days.

7
DRINKS

Hot and cold drinks in India are a big deal. There is no tradition of drinking alcoholic beverages with food and so this is not generally the area in which Indians show flair and passion. In fact, Indians don't ferment their food and water to purify it in the same way as in the West. Alcohol can also make hot food taste hideously hotter. With meals, we drink water, just water. This perceived alliance of curry and beer is something we Indians don't recognise.

Lassi is the big drink on the Indian street food scene. It is a yogurt-based cooler. In the heat of the Indian streets, people can lose fluid and electrolytes through perspiration. The most popular lassi is thus a salted one. It contains ground roasted cumin and salt and performs the function of an electrolytic rebalancer. It's funny, on the streets of Leicester a salted masala lassi is the last thing I want to drink, but on a hot Varanasi afternoon, I crave them.

In Mowgli I had some fun with the lassi flavours. Mango is very popular and so this was something of a no-brainer. My children drink their own weight in it when they go to the restaurant and for that reason alone it will aways remain. My personal favourite is the highly floral and fragrant Rose and Cardamom Lassi, which is sweet but so very exotic and other worldly. Lassis are great opportunities to play fast and loose with soft fruit and all things pulpable. Very often Indian restaurants are judged by their lassi. I don't want to taste condensed milk. The balance of sweet, sharp and a touch of savoury is important. My mother would never make a sweet lassi without adding a pinch of salt.

Indians also love hot drinks, and spiced masala tea is the way in which Indians love to finish a meal. The tea tends to be very milky and sweet. The spices are infused and the tea leaves are strong and aromatic. There is a charm in the Indian way of serving these hot drinks in fine small clay pots. The pots absorb a little of the water and so the tea intensifies in its perfume and sweetness.

187

MANGO LASSI

Try to get hold of Alphonso or Kesar mangoes for this lassi to taste really authentic. With the big, shop-bought mangoes of the West you get a very different, though still lovely drink. Mango lassi is the drink of choice of most of our Indian clients. I make it with soy milk and low-fat yogurt to keep it light and leave more room for food.

200g/7oz very ripe mango	2 tbsp plain yogurt	juice of ½ lime
	2 tbsp soy milk	⅛ tsp salt

1 Peel the mango by cutting away the fatter sides from the stone/pit, then carefully cut crosses into the flesh and turn inside out so the cubes of mango are sticking out. Use a tablespoon to scoop the mango out and into a blender.

2 Add the yogurt, soy milk, lime juice and salt and blend until smooth. Add a little water to thin down to your taste if necessary.

PINEAPPLE, CHILLI & LIME LASSI

This is the closest you will get to the very basic sweetened, sharpened, salted yogurt drink from the streets of India. This drink takes me back to my childhood visits to the lassi capital, Varanasi – hot, bustling dust punctuated with this soothing, refreshing ambrosia.

2 tbsp pineapple juice	juice of ½ lime	60ml/2fl oz/¼ cup soy milk
2½ tsp agave syrup	140g/4½oz/generous	
¼ bird's-eye chilli	½ cup plain yogurt	⅛ tsp salt

1 Put all the ingredients into a blender and blend until smooth. Add a little water to thin down to your taste if necessary.

LYCHEE LASSI

Canned lychees really do work best with this drink. Use the syrup and blend that in with the yogurt too. This adds a lot of flavour and also much of the sweetness. Lychees need blending very well as they can be fibrous. Don't expect the smoothest drink, but do expect a wonderful floral, fresh sweetness.

200g/7oz canned lychees
140g/4½oz/generous ½ cup
    plain yogurt

60ml/2fl oz/¼ cup soy milk
juice of ½ lime
pinch of salt

1 Put all the ingredients into a blender and blend until smooth. Add a little water to thin down to your taste if necessary.

ROSE & CARDAMOM LASSI

This is made beautifully pink by adding the sweet sharpness of grenadine. It's a very sweet lassi, rather like a Middle Eastern sweet rose sherbert, but in the form of a yogurt-based cooler. Because of this floral, heady sweetness, the grenadine is critical to sharpen the drink and kick it awake. If you can't get any, blend in a handful of raspberries as they have a similar effect.

⅛ tsp rosewater
1 tbsp Green Cardamom
    Extract (see page 215)
1 tsp grenadine

125g/4oz/½ cup plain
    yogurt
75ml/2½fl oz/⅓ cup
    soy milk

¼ tsp caster/granulated
    sugar
pinch of salt

1 Put all the ingredients into a blender and blend until smooth. Add a little water to thin down to your taste if necessary.

Recipes pictured overleaf from left to right

STRAWBERRY AND MINT LASSI

Strawberries don't really happen in India. No, we have the wrong climate over there. They are to me the wonderful flavour of all things British. This is a lassi I love to make in the summer when strawberries are as fresh and sweet as sunshine. Feel free to use canned or frozen berries when you need to stock up on vitamin D in the bleak midwinter.

200g/7oz fresh strawberries
2 sprigs of fresh mint
juice of ½ lime

125g/4oz/½ cup plain yogurt
60ml/2fl oz/¼ cup soy milk
pinch of salt

1 Put all the ingredients into a blender and blend until smooth. Add a little water to thin down to your taste if necessary.

192

CARDAMOM COFFEE

Cardamom and coffee are a wonderfully synergistic combination of flavours. Remember it is always green cardamom pods that you use in dessert or sweet dishes. They are much more perfumed than the older, gnarled black ones and make a mundane early morning coffee so very exotic and full of promise.

2 heaped tsp fresh medium-ground coffee

2 green cardamom pods, crushed

1 Take your cafetière/French press and place it on a steady, flat surface, then remove the plunger.

2 Add your freshly ground coffee and crushed green cardamom pods, then carefully pour in 400ml/14fl oz/1⅔ cups water, just off the boil.

3 Stir gently for 30 seconds, then reinsert the plunger so that it stops just above the water and coffee. Let the coffee stand for 4–5 minutes.

193

4 Press the plunger down slowly, making sure to exert an even, steady pressure. Pour into cups and serve.

MASALA TEA

This is a tea that we often drink when we feel a cold coming on. We boil up the spices with the bracing strong tea and then usually add heaps of sugar and milk as is the wont of many an Indian. There is probably little evidence for its medicinal value, but emotionally it works for me every time!

2 green cardamom pods

1 clove

6cm/2½ inch piece of fresh root ginger

1 tsp assam tea

125ml/4fl oz/½ cup almond milk

1 tbsp honey

1 Add the cardamom pods, clove and fresh root ginger to a pestle and mortar and grind into a coarse paste, then set aside.

2 Add 150ml/5fl oz/⅔ cup water to a small saucepan set over a medium heat and bring up to the boil. Add the crushed spices, boil for 2 minutes, then reduce the heat to low.

3 Add the assam tea and simmer gently for 2–5 minutes (the time depends on how strong you want the tea to be).

4 Add the almond milk and honey and continue to simmer for a further 2 minutes. Taste and add more honey if you prefer a sweeter tea.

5 Strain through a fine mesh strainer into a mug.

GINGER TEA

This is something my Singaporean Indian friend used to make for me when we went to visit. The more ginger for me, the better. It's almost like a hot ginger-beer float. Great for sore throats and feels rather cleansing.

½ tbsp fresh root ginger, peeled and grated

½ tbsp honey

juice of ¼ lemon

sprig of fresh mint

small pinch of cayenne pepper

1 Add 250ml/9fl oz/1 cup water to a small saucepan set over a medium heat and bring up to the boil. Add all of the ingredients, stir well, then remove from the heat and cover with a lid. Allow to steep for 10 minutes.

2 Strain through a fine mesh strainer before serving.

HIBISCUS TEA

Hibiscus flowers have a sour flavour that always surprises me. They are so pretty and yet so tart. They give little by way of floral hue and so the orange blossom water and honey is needed to make your brain not feel short-changed.

10g/½oz dried hibiscus flowers

½ small cinnamon stick

½ tsp orange blossom water

2 tbsp honey

½ lime

ice

1 Place all the ingredients in a large bowl with 500ml/17fl oz/2 cups water and mix well, then cover and refrigerate for at least 8 hours.

2 Pass through a fine mesh strainer and taste, adding more honey to sweeten if necessary.

3 Serve over ice.

CHAI LATTE

PREP: 5 MINUTES • COOK: 15 MINUTES • SERVES 1

This drink has its roots in the homes and streets of India. It is very normal for us to add spices to our tea to give flavour and, we believe, a little medicinal value. Tea in India is usually very milky and sweet and this balances the spices. It has all the hit of a spiced rice pudding, but in the form of a bracing brew. I use almond milk in this recipe to make it lighter, but feel free to use full-cream/whole cows' milk, which is heavier, but more authentic.

½ tbsp black loose-leaf tea (or 2 black
 tea bags)
1 tsp ground cinnamon
½ tsp ground ginger
¼ tsp freshly ground black pepper

¼ tsp ground cloves
¼ tsp ground cardamom
½ tbsp honey
125ml/4fl oz/½ cup almond milk

1 Put the black tea and ground spices in a small saucepan set over a medium heat, add 200ml/7fl oz/scant 1 cup water and bring up to the boil. Reduce the heat and simmer gently for 15 minutes, allowing the tea and spices to steep. Remove from the heat and allow to cool slightly for a few minutes.

2 Add the honey and almond milk and stir well. Taste and add a little more honey if you prefer your tea a little sweeter, then pour through a fine mesh strainer into a mug.

TURMERIC LATTE

In India we call this *haldi doodh*. It is very simple and involves milk and turmeric. We drink it for its health-giving properties and it has become the new big fad in the West. To make it sweet and more multi-dimensional in flavour, we add ginger and cinnamon to almond milk as a base.

250ml/9fl oz/1 cup almond milk
1½ tsp ground turmeric
½ tsp ground cinnamon
1 tbsp fresh root ginger, peeled
 and grated

1 tbsp honey
pinch of freshly ground black pepper

1 Heat the almond milk gently in a small saucepan set over a medium heat, taking care not to boil.

2 Add the turmeric, cinnamon, ginger, honey and black pepper and whisk gently until light and foamy. Pour into a mug and serve hot.

197

8
THE COCKTAIL CAGE

The Cocktail Cage of Mowgli really trapped me ideologically for a while. The truth is on the streets and in the homes of India, people do not drink alcohol with their food. I'm not saying they are not drinkers, no sir. My father and his peers would happily pickle themselves with Johnnie Walker Black Label and my mother struggles to walk past Merlot, but with their food, absolutely not. This is one of the reasons that I refused to have an Indian beer on the menu. There is no such thing. We drink water with our meals, not beer. Alcoholic drinks irritate the palate that is already being assaulted by spices and chilli acids.

Cocktails are such a beautiful thing when done well. This was my dilemma. I love the alchemy of pairing interesting spices and ingredients with the towering punch of Western spirits. To me, the cocktail kitchen was one in which food ingredients took precedence. Herbs, spices, fruits and syrups were not the tail wagging the dog, but the dog, the absolute dog. This to me was justification for the development of the Mowgli Cocktail Cage. Within it, I must always be shackled to that which is at the heart of Mowgli – the clever use of good ingredients. It does, however, make us outward facing and gives our clients a different dimension in which to enjoy our spice wielding.

When I first opened Mowgli in Liverpool, a most charismatic and virtuosic cocktail king and friend, Danny Murphy, had the kindness and good grace to guide us through his cocktail runes. He taught us the dark arts of extracting haunting strains from our exotic ingredients and capturing them in fiery spirits, rather in the way that our food captures them in oils and marinades.

Danny trained us all in what clients need to see and need to taste in the most iconic of cocktails. He taught us how to have fun behind the bar and how to be brave with our spirits. His spirit has never left us and he gave our Mowgli monkey tails an extra flick of sass.

MOWGLI GIN & TONIC

I always wanted a gin and tonic for Mowgli that spoke of coriander/cilantro. I love the sheer taste of green in this cocktail. It's one of our big sellers and feels like a summer's day with the windows flung open onto verdant meadows.

2cm/¾ inch piece of fresh root ginger, peeled and sliced
2 fresh coriander/cilantro stalks
40ml/1¼fl oz gin
4 tsp lime juice
4 tsp Gomme (see page 214)

ice cubes and crushed ice
125ml/4fl oz tonic water

FOR THE GARNISH
slice of fresh root ginger
1 lime wedge

1 In a cocktail shaker, muddle the fresh root ginger and coriander stalks – this helps to bring their flavours out.

2 Add the gin, lime juice and gomme, then fill the cocktail shaker with ice cubes and shake vigorously for 6 seconds.

3 Fill a collins glass to the top with crushed ice, then strain the cocktail into the glass, adding enough tonic to suit your taste. Finish by garnishing with a slice of fresh root ginger and wedge of lime.

202

ROSE & RASPBERRY GIN & TONIC

I got the idea for this blend of ingredients from a jam I picked up at a farmers' market. I found it so sweet that I couldn't taste the rose. It was overpowered. I thought gin would be a good sharpening breakwater between sweetness and fragrance. It works so well. Each flavour flows through in waves. Simple and superb.

35ml/1¼fl oz gin

4 tsp Raspberry and Ginger Purée (see page 216)

1 tbsp gomme (see page 214)

1 tbsp lime juice

1 tsp rosewater

ice cubes

125ml/4fl oz tonic water

FOR THE GARNISH

1 fresh raspberry

1 small pinch of dried rose petals

1 Put the gin, purée, gomme, lime juice, rosewater and ice cubes into a cocktail shaker and shake vigorously for 6 seconds.

2 Fill a collins glass with ice, then strain the cocktail into the glass and top up with tonic.

3 Finish by garnishing with a fresh raspberry and a pinch of dried rose petals.

203

SWEET DELHI DIAZEPAM

PREP: 5 MINUTES • SERVES 1

This is the Mowgli lady in red. Raspberry, passion fruit, herby chartreuse – it is all things to all people. This is one of those drinks that if one passes, no *sashays*, through the restaurant on a tray, then everyone orders one. It just looks like a party in a glass.

25ml/1fl oz Raspberry and Ginger
    Purée (see page 216)
30ml/1fl oz gin
2 tsp green chartreuse
2 tsp passion fruit syrup
4 tsp lemon juice

60ml/2fl oz/¼ cup apple juice
ice cubes and crushed ice

FOR THE GARNISH
1 lemon wedge
1 fresh raspberry

1 Put all the ingredients into a cocktail shaker and fill with ice cubes, then shake vigorously for 6 seconds.

2 Fill a glass of your choice to the top with crushed ice, then strain and pour the cocktail over the ice and into the glass.

3 Finish by garnishing with a lemon wedge and a fresh raspberry.

204

KERALAN SOUTHSIDE

PREP: 5 MINUTES • SERVES 1

OK, so this is my favourite cocktail. The Keralan Southside is a good test of restraint and delicacy in the hands of the mixologist. We use kaffir lime leaves in this along with fresh mint. It is so herbal and elegant. Use fresh lime leaves for the best effect.

4 kaffir lime leaves
10 fresh mint leaves
ice cubes

50ml/2fl oz gin
2 tbsp lemon juice
2 tbsp Gomme (see page 214)

1 In a cocktail shaker add the kaffir lime leaves, mint leaves and a couple of ice cubes and shake vigorously for 6 seconds – this helps the leaves to release their flavour.

2 Next add the gin, lemon juice and gomme and shake for a further 6 seconds, then strain into a chilled glass.

CHAI RUM SLING

I remember sitting in the window of Bold Street Mowgli in the early days working my socks off on some spreadsheet or other. Danny Miceli, one of our beloved bar backs, affectionately brought me this pick-me-up that he had devised. I loved it. It was sweet, spiced, fresh and happy in so many ways. It had to make the menu.

10 fresh mint leaves

4 tsp lime juice

3 tsp Gomme (see page 214)

2 tsp apricot liqueur

40ml/1¼fl oz Chai Rum (see page 216)

60ml/2fl oz/¼ cup apple juice

ice cubes and crushed ice

FOR THE GARNISH

couple of sprigs of fresh mint

1 lime wedge

1 Clap the mint leaves between your hands to help them release their flavour. Add with all the other ingredients into a cocktail shaker and fill with ice cubes, close the shaker tightly and give it a vigorous shake for 6 seconds.

2 Fill a glass to the top with crushed ice, then pour the cocktail into the glass through a strainer. Finish by garnishing with a couple of sprigs of fresh mint and a wedge of lime.

TEQUILA, PINEAPPLE, CHILLI & LIME LASSI

PREP: 5 MINUTES • SERVES 1

The fresh chilli hit at the back of this lassi made it an obvious vehicle for a good shot of tequila. The combination of flavours is lovely, and cheeky. There is a sweet slow start and then the double kick at the end with the heat of Mexico flowing through an Indian staple.

15ml/½fl oz blanco tequila
250ml/8fl oz/1 cup Pineapple, Chilli
    and Lime Lassi (see page 188)

FOR THE GARNISH
pinch of dried chilli/hot pepper flakes

 In a glass of your choice add the tequila, then pour over the lassi and give a small stir with a teaspoon. Finish by garnishing with a small sprinkle of chilli flakes

MOWGLI PENICILLIN

PREP: 5 MINUTES • SERVES 1

This is a real tonic. The Mowgli Penicillin is the cocktail-makers' cocktail. It is one that only those in the know order. When Mowgli first opened, other bartenders would come by stealth and test us with this drink. Thankfully the best of them, my friend Danny Murphy, the Liverpool cocktail demigod, designed this one for me. His association with our cocktail kitchen is what placed us beyond reproach.

50g/2oz stem ginger
40ml/1¼fl oz bourbon whiskey
15ml/½fl oz peaty single malt whisky,
    such as Ardbeg
4 tsp lemon juice

2 tsp honey
2 tsp Raspberry and Ginger Purée
    (see page 216)
ice cubes

1 Put the stem ginger in a blender and pour over a little water just to cover. Blend until it forms a smooth purée, then set aside.

2 Next put the bourbon, whisky, lemon juice, honey and raspberry and ginger purée into a cocktail shaker, fill with ice cubes and shake vigorously for 6 seconds.

3 Pour the cocktail through a double strainer into a chilled coupe glass.

SMOKED CARDAMOM OLD-FASHIONED

The old-fashioned is such a hard drink to get right. It is the benchmark of a good whiskey kitchen. We cook ours up with the smoked essence of black cardamom, which has an almost medicinal edge. The apricot liqueur sweetens the bitter pill. The food critic, Giles Coren, called this the best f****** old-fashioned he had ever had. Shame he had to swear. I couldn't show my mum his tweet.

40ml/1¼fl oz Curry Shoulder
   (see page 217)
2 tsp apricot liqueur
2 tsp Black Cardamom Gomme
   (see page 215)

2 dashes of Angostura Bitters
ice cubes

FOR THE GARNISH
2 curry leaves
1 black cardamom pod

210

1 Put all the ingredients straight into your glass, then fill three-quarters full with ice cubes.

2 Stir using a teaspoon for 10 seconds, then fill the glass to just below the rim with more ice.

3 Finish by garnishing with the fresh curry leaves and black cardamom pod.

LYCHEE ROSE MARTINI

This is such a beautiful and precious cocktail to me. It is my mother's favourite. The problem is that she does knock them back... They are so floral and light and the combination of lychee and rose is uniquely sublime. We use a dried edible rose petal garnish. You can use whole fresh rose petals to pretty it up even more.

50ml/2fl oz vodka
50ml/2fl oz lychee juice
25ml/1fl oz lemon juice
25ml/1fl oz Rose Gomme (see page 214)

ice cubes

FOR THE GARNISH
couple of dried rose petals

1 Put all the ingredients in a cocktail shaker and fill with ice, then shake vigorously for 6 seconds.

2 Strain and pour into a chilled coupette glass, then finish by garnishing with a couple of dried rose petals

213

COCKTAIL COMPONENTS

There are two advantages to Mowgli-fying your cocktails. One is that they will taste immense, and I mean magically immense. The second is that you can array your shelves with the most fascinating and exotic jars of steeping loveliness. Rather like the mystical picklings of an Eastern antique apothecary, these ingredients don't just taste mesmerising, but look enticingly come-hither.

GOMME

PREP: 5 MINUTES • COOK: 5 MINUTES • MAKES 2 CUPS

Gommes are flavoured syrups that are like a parfum honey. The power is in the length of the steep. A few drops add sweetness and spiced flavour to your cocktails.

1kg/2lb 3oz/4½ cups sugar

1 Set a small saucepan over a low heat and add the sugar and 500ml/17fl oz/2 cups water. Stir, then simmer gently, taking care not to boil, until the sugar has fully dissolved. Store in an airtight bottle for up to a month.

ROSE GOMME

PREP: 5 MINUTES • COOK: 5 MINUTES • MAKES 2 CUPS

1kg/2lb 3oz/4½ cups sugar
2½ tbsp rosewater
50g/2oz dried rose petals

1 Set a small saucepan over a low heat and add the sugar, rosewater, dried rose petals and 500ml/17fl oz/2 cups water. Stir, then simmer gently, taking care not to boil, until the sugar has fully dissolved. Remove from the heat and let cool completely.

2 Strain and store in an airtight bottle for up to a month.

BLACK CARDAMOM GOMME

PREP: 5 MINUTES + 1 WEEK STEEPING • MAKES 2 CUPS

150g/5oz smoked black cardamom pods
500ml/17fl oz/2 cups Gomme (see recipe opposite)

1 Combine the black cardamom pods and gomme in an airtight container and leave to steep for at least a week. The longer it's left, the better it gets.

GREEN CARDAMOM EXTRACT

PREP: 10 MINUTES + 12 HOURS STEEPING • MAKES 4 CUPS

The green cardamom extract really captures the essence of the Indian dessert kitchen. Green, not black, cardamom is the spice of the sweet meats. Hence it works so well in our gomme-infused cocktails

100g/3½oz green cardamom pods
3 cardamom tea bags

1 Put the green cardamom pods and tea bags in a small mixing bowl, then cover with boiling water and mix with a spoon. Leave to stand for 5 minutes, then top up with more boiling water until you have 1 litre/35fl oz/4¼ cups of water in the bowl.

2 Cover and leave to steep for 12 hours, then strain and store in an airtight container for up to a month.

RASPBERRY AND GINGER PURÉE

We use lots of raspberry and ginger purée in Mowgli. Fresh, zesty ingredients, blended together, add the tart heat and colour to cocktails like the Sweet Delhi Diazepam (see page 204) and the Rose & Raspberry Gin & Tonic (see page 203).

100g/3½oz stem ginger
400g/14oz fresh raspberries

1 Put the ingredients in a food processor with 3 tablespoons boiling water and blend until they form a smooth paste. Store in an airtight container for up to 3 days.

CHAI RUM

PREP: 5 MINUTES + 6 HOURS STEEPING • MAKES 3 CUPS

Chai Rum has a mulled, Christmas spice-nose and works very well in a sweet long cocktail.

700ml/24fl oz/3 cups white rum
20g/¾oz loose-leaf chai or 15 chai tea bags
20g/¾oz cinnamon sticks

1 Put the white rum, chai tea and cinnamon sticks in a mixing bowl, then cover and leave to steep for 6 hours, stirring regularly.

2 Strain and store in an airtight container for up to a month.

CURRY SHOULDER

Curry Shoulder is our infusion of whisky with curry leaves. There is a natural smoky aroma in the curry leaves that almost emulates the peat smoke edge of a good whisky.

700ml/24fl oz/3 cups bourbon whiskey
30g/1oz fresh curry leaves, stalks and stems removed

1 Put the bourbon and fresh curry leaves in a mixing bowl, then cover and leave to steep for 48 hours.

2 Strain and store in an airtight container for up to 2 months.

INDEX

219

223

ACKNOWLEDGMENTS

Thanks will always go to Maa, the High Priest of Mowgli. To Nik, my big brother, who had my back and sanity when I abandoned identity, salary and security to build Mowgli. To AK and Monmon for encouragement when we were very scared and very skint, with only a set of pans and a dream.

Love to Shona, Mirren, Nayan, Eila, Honour, Willow, Atticus, Mochi, Foofi, Mike and Den, the Mowgli menu guinea pigs who fill my hall with shoes and my kitchen with laughter.

When writing a book, your publisher becomes a literary sibling and playtime was such fun with the brilliant Kate Fox, thank you. Glen, Yuki and Aya, thanks for bringing my vision and food alive.

These recipes are the legacy I leave, not just to India and Tia but to all of you who are good enough to support Mowgli by dining with us. I never thought she would survive. I risked my all to build her and I built her in order to present to you the dishes I have eaten all my life. Now they are yours. May your house smell like my Maa's, may your kitchens glow forever with turmeric sunshine and may your work become your passion and joy as it has for me.

For these blessings I am most grateful.